100
THINGS TO
KNOW ABOUT
PLANET
EARTH

Usborne Quicklinks

For links to websites and video clips where you can find out more about many of the facts in this book, and discover even more about our amazing planet, go to the Usborne Quicklinks website at **usborne.com/Quicklinks** and enter the keywords: **things to know about planet earth**.

Here are some of the things you can do at the websites we recommend:

- Find out more about the long migrations made by animals, including butterflies and crabs
- Watch a video clip about the wolves that changed the course of a river
- Listen to the sound of singing sand
- See stunning photos of the Cave of Crystals in Mexico
- Explore the rainforest growing inside the world's largest cave
- Find out more about the unique wildlife of Madagascar

Please follow the online safety guidelines at the Usborne Quicklinks website. Children should be supervised online.

100
THINGS TO
KNOW ABOUT

PLANET
EARTH

Written by
Jerome Martin, Darran Stobbart,
Alice James and Tom Mumbray

Illustrated by
Federico Mariani, Parko Polo
and Dale Edwin Murray

Layout and design by
Jenny Offley, Lenka Hrehova
and Tilly Kitching

With expert advice from
Dr. Roger Trend

1 Africa is bigger... or smaller...

than Greenland – depending on your map.

Mapmakers face a tricky problem: how to show the Earth, which is ball-shaped, as a flat map on paper. There are many methods, but none of them can get everything quite right.

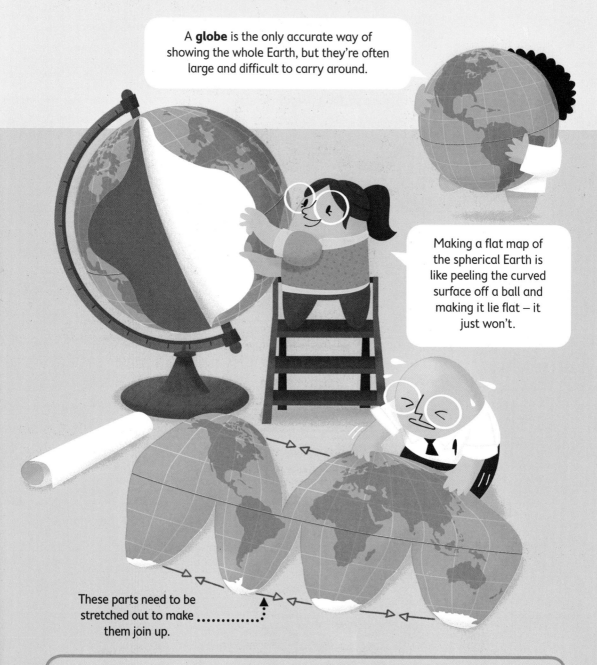

A **globe** is the only accurate way of showing the whole Earth, but they're often large and difficult to carry around.

Making a flat map of the spherical Earth is like peeling the curved surface off a ball and making it lie flat — it just won't.

These parts need to be stretched out to make them join up.

You can find a map of lots of the places mentioned in this book on pages 120-121.
For a list of terms, go to the glossary on pages 124-125.

Mapmakers use different ways of stretching and squashing their maps to make them flat. These are known as **projections**.

The **Mercator projection** was created by Dutch mapmaker Gerardus Mercator in 1569. The *shapes* of the countries are fairly accurate...

...but *sizes* of those at the top and bottom appear much bigger than they really are.

The **Gall-Peters projection** was first created by James Gall in 1855. It keeps the *sizes* of all the countries correct in relation to each other...

...but this means their *shapes* are squashed and stretched.

Africa (shown in green) is actually 14 times bigger than Greenland (shown in purple), but here's how they compare on different maps.

Mercator (accurate shapes, inaccurate sizes)

Accurate size comparison and actual shapes

Gall-Peters (accurate sizes, shapes distorted)

Even digital maps of the world viewed on a computer screen can't overcome this problem.

2 Shadows and a camel...

are all you need to measure the Earth.

In ancient times, no one knew the size of the Earth. But around 2,300 years ago, a Greek mathematician named Eratosthenes came up with a simple method to find out – and his results were surprisingly accurate.

Eratosthenes noticed that at midday, buildings of the same height cast shadows of *different* lengths in *different* cities.

Alexandria

Syene

He hired someone to ride a camel from Alexandria to Syene to measure the distance between them.

Alexandria

Syene

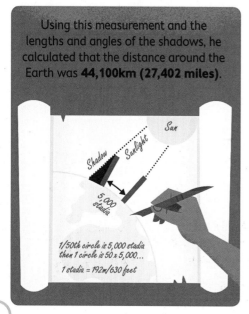

Using this measurement and the lengths and angles of the shadows, he calculated that the distance around the Earth was **44,100km (27,402 miles)**.

Sun

Shadow   Sunlight

5,000 stadia

1/50th circle is 5,000 stadia
then 1 circle is 50 x 5,000...

1 stadia = 192m/630 feet

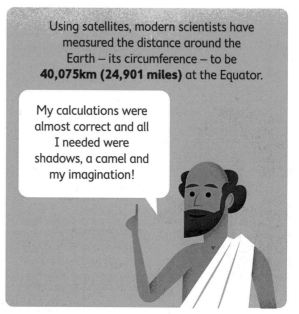

Using satellites, modern scientists have measured the distance around the Earth – its circumference – to be **40,075km (24,901 miles)** at the Equator.

My calculations were almost correct and all I needed were shadows, a camel and my imagination!

3 Conditions on Earth...

are *just right* for life.

Earth orbits the Sun in what astronomers call the **Goldilocks Zone**, where just enough sunlight reaches the planet to make conditions *just right* for life. So far, it's the only place we know of where life has developed at all.

What makes Earth so perfect?

Liquid water

Earth's distance from the Sun makes it warm enough to have liquid water on its surface at all times. This is vital for life. Closer, the water would boil off; further away, the planet would freeze to death.

Shifting continents

The Earth's crust is constantly shifting. This redistributes and recycles important elements for life, including carbon and iron.

Enough atmosphere

Earth's size means that it has enough gravity to hold on to its atmosphere. This shields the planet from deadly radiation from space.

This planet is **just right!**

However – just because Earth is the only planet where we've seen life thrive, it doesn't mean it's the only one in the universe.

4 Two dozen rabbits...

changed the landscape of Australia.

When a new species (type) of animal or plant arrives in an area, it can upset the balance of local wildlife. These newcomers are known as an **invasive species**. This is what happened with just 24 rabbits...

Although he wasn't the first to introduce rabbits to Australia, the problem seems to have begun in 1859, when an English settler named Thomas Austin released **24 rabbits** onto his estate...

Those rabbits bred...

...and bred...

...and bred.

Between 1901 and 1907, over 3,000km (1,900 miles) of fencing was built to stop the rabbits from spreading. The plan failed: the rabbits simply dug under the fences.

In just 60 years, the country's rabbit population soared to an estimated **10 billion**.

They munched their way through grass, small plants and young trees. They even ate the roots, stopping new plants from growing and leaving little food for the native animals.

With no plants to protect the soil, the wind blew it away, and areas previously covered in vegetation became barren.

Rabbits remain an invasive species in Australia today, and their numbers have to be kept under control by the government.

5 Water, water everywhere...

but barely a drop to drink.

Earth is often described as the **blue planet** because 70% of its surface is covered in water. But in relation to the volume of the *whole* Earth there really isn't much water at all – and most is too salty for people to drink.

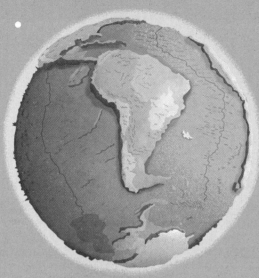

Most of the inside of the planet is made from solid rock and molten rock known as **magma**.

By **volume** all of the water on Earth makes up just 0.02% of the planet.

6 Nets, ropes and plastic bags...

were found inside a whale.

When a young sperm whale washed up on a Spanish beach in 2018, all sorts of man-made objects were found inside its stomach, including 30kg (66lb) of plastic...

Experts think that eating all this waste damaged the whale's digestive system, and killed it.

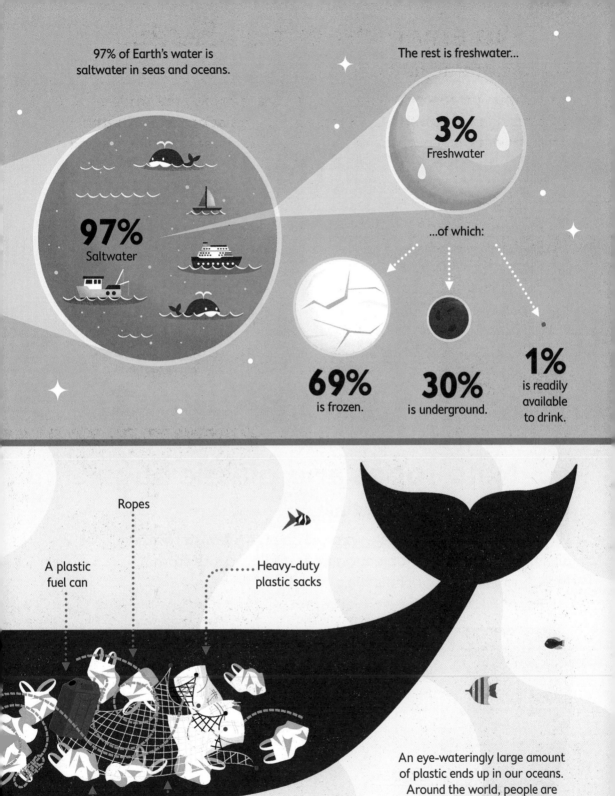

97% of Earth's water is saltwater in seas and oceans.

The rest is freshwater...

3%
Freshwater

97%
Saltwater

...of which:

69%
is frozen.

30%
is underground.

1%
is readily available to drink.

Ropes

A plastic fuel can

Heavy-duty plastic sacks

An eye-wateringly large amount of plastic ends up in our oceans. Around the world, people are dumping the equivalent of one waste truck full of plastic into the ocean every minute.

Dozens of plastic shopping bags

Nets

7 No environment on Earth...

is too extreme for bacteria.

Bacteria are microscopic organisms. They are among the smallest and toughest life forms on Earth. Some species are at home in extreme environments, places that are inhospitable to most other life, including...

...frozen in the Arctic ice.

...inside the human body.

...inside solid rock.

...the deepest part of the ocean.

...on hailstones.

Scientists call life forms that live in difficult environments such as these **extremophiles**.

8 All the bacteria on Earth...

outweigh all the human beings.

Bacteria are so small that 10,000 of them could fit on the tip of a pencil. But, because there are so many bacteria on the planet, together they outweigh humans by an incomprehensible amount.

Average weight
of a single bacterium:
0.000000000000000665kg
(0.0000000000000001466lb)

Different types of bacteria vary in weight, but this is the weight of single *E. coli* bacterium.

Average weight of an
adult human:
62kg (137lb)

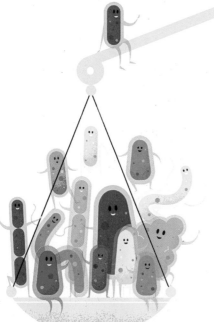

There are more than
7,800,000,000 people
on the planet, but
there are an estimated
**5,000,000,000,000,000,
000,000,000,000,000**
individual bacteria in the
world – that's five followed
by **thirty zeroes**.

All of this adds up to bacteria outweighing humans by a massive amount. And that's good news for the planet. Many species of bacteria play an important role, breaking down and recycling elements in the soil and oceans to keep them healthy.

9 Deserts bloom with flowers...

after rainstorms.

Deserts are the driest places on Earth – but many plant species still find a way to survive. Their seeds need water to grow, but they remain inactive under the ground for years, waiting for the rains to come.

The Atacama Desert in South America can get as little as **1mm (0.04 inches)** of rain a year.

Every 5-7 years, heavy rainfall hits the area.

The rain makes the seeds burst into life.

Within just a few days flowers burst into bloom, covering the usually bleak landscape.

These desert blooms last for several weeks before the plants die, leaving new seeds behind, ready for the next rains...

10 Shyness...

prevents some trees from touching.

If you look from the ground up at the tree tops of particular forests, you'll see little gaps between the leaves and branches of separate trees. This is caused by a phenomenon known as **crown shyness**.

The top of a tree is called a **crown**.

Trees' leafy crowns grow around each other.

The types of trees that do this are found across different continents. The reason may be to stop leaf-eating insects from moving from tree to tree...

...or a response to trees hitting against each other in windy places.

11 The Great Dying...

killed almost all the species in the sea.

About 250 million years ago, a staggering 96% of the species in Earth's seas and oceans died out. Scientists call this event the **Permian Extinction**, or **Great Dying**.

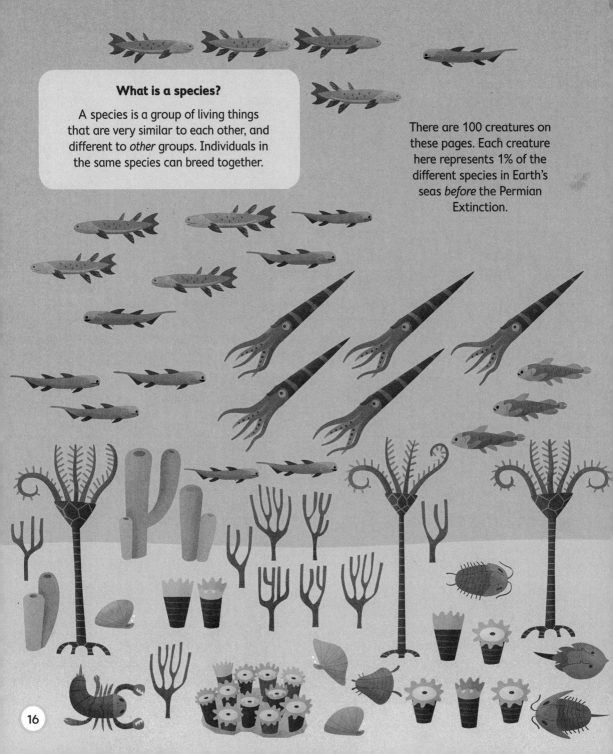

What is a species?

A species is a group of living things that are very similar to each other, and different to *other* groups. Individuals in the same species can breed together.

There are 100 creatures on these pages. Each creature here represents 1% of the different species in Earth's seas *before* the Permian Extinction.

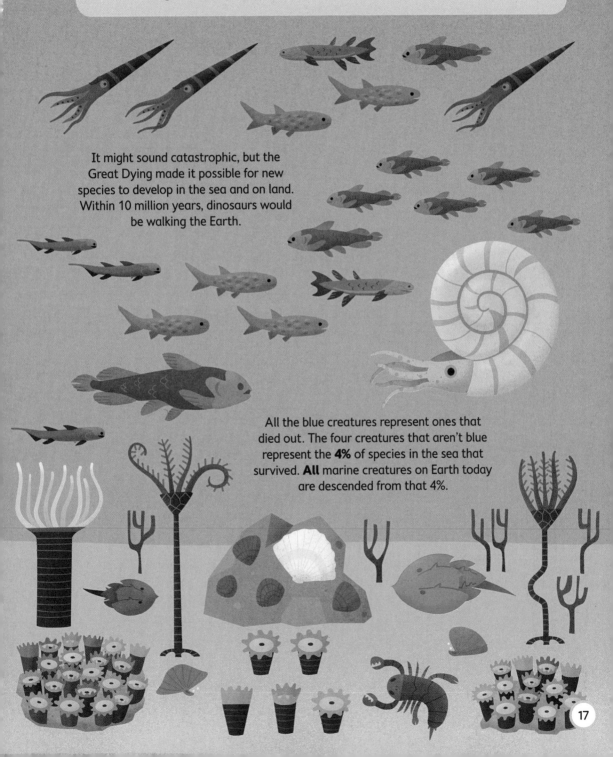

What might have caused the Great Dying?

An asteroid hitting the Earth?

A huge release of methane gas that had been trapped under the sea?

Huge volcanic eruptions?

These are some of the theories, but scientists don't know if it was one, a combination, or something else altogether.

It might sound catastrophic, but the Great Dying made it possible for new species to develop in the sea and on land. Within 10 million years, dinosaurs would be walking the Earth.

All the blue creatures represent ones that died out. The four creatures that aren't blue represent the **4%** of species in the sea that survived. **All** marine creatures on Earth today are descended from that 4%.

17

We're living in an ice age...

but it won't last much longer.

The Earth's climate has been changing and shifting since the planet formed. There have been boiling oceans of molten rock, and freezing, glacial ice ages, the most recent of which is still going on. This page shows how the climate has changed throughout the Earth's history, from 4.6 billion years ago up to the present day.

bya = billions of years ago
mya = millions of years ago

Very hot (above 90°C, 194°F)	Hot (26-89°C, 79-192°F)	Mid (16-25°C, 61-77°F)	Cool (0-15°C, 32-59°F)	Ice age (below 0°C, 32°F)

Each band represents **10 million years** of Earth's history.

4.6bya
Earth forms – hot, molten and volcanic

3.5bya
First life appears – a tiny, algae-like organism

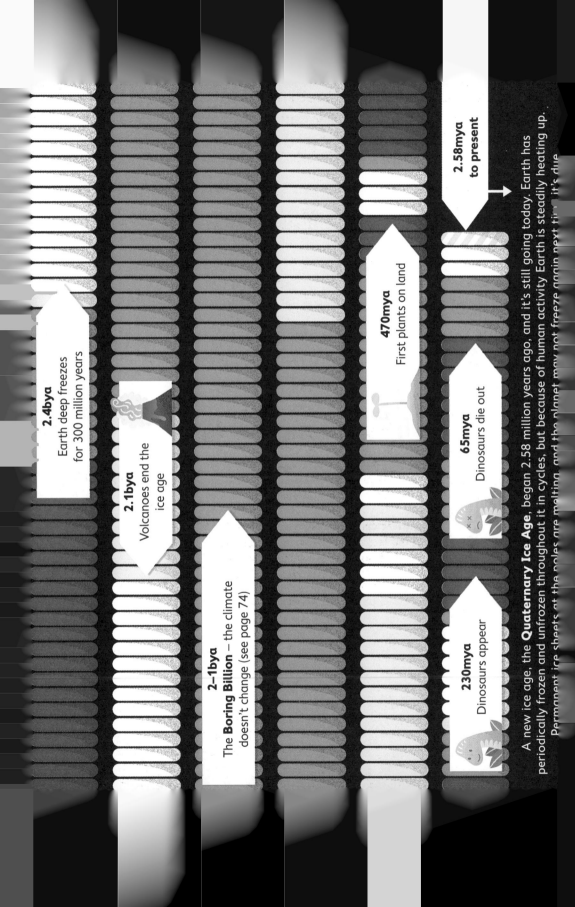

2.4bya
Earth deep freezes
for 300 million years

2.1bya
Volcanoes end the
ice age

2–1bya
The **Boring Billion** – the climate
doesn't change (see page 74)

470mya
First plants on land

230mya
Dinosaurs appear

65mya
Dinosaurs die out

**2.58mya
to present**

A new ice age, the **Quaternary Ice Age**, began 2.58 million years ago, and it's still going today. Earth has periodically frozen and unfrozen throughout it in cycles, but because of human activity Earth is steadily heating up. Permanent ice sheets at the poles are melting, and the planet may not freeze again next time it's due.

13 To experience Mars on Earth...

scientists visit the Atacama Desert.

The Atacama Desert, in Chile, in South America, is one of the oldest and driest deserts on the planet. Rocky, barren and inhospitable, it bears an uncanny resemblance to the surface of Mars.

The Atacama desert is made mainly of parched, rocky, salty soil, ancient lava flows, and dried-up lake beds.

In fact, it resembles Mars so closely that scientists use it to test out their new robot rovers.

It's like I'm already there!

How dry is the Atacama Desert?
The region has been a desert for over **10 million years**. In some places, there is no sign that rain has *ever* fallen.

A double shadow

The high mountain ranges on either side of the Atacama Desert block rain clouds from passing over. This creates especially dry areas known as **rain shadows**.

Moist air

Dry air

Dry air

Moist air

Double rain shadow

Pacific Ocean

Chilean Coast Range

Atacama Desert

Andes Mountains

If any life exists on Mars, it is likely to take the form of **microbes** — simple, microscopic organisms — sheltering underground.

Such microbes can also be found in the soil of the Atacama Desert. So scientists also come here to test drilling and sampling tools that they hope to use some day on Mars.

Life in the fog

At the edge of the Atacama Desert, fog often creeps in from the Pacific Ocean. Here, a few desert plants have adapted to survive by catching and sucking moisture from the fog.

Galactic views

The night sky over the Atacama Desert is clear, dry, free of pollution and very dark — so it's an ideal place to build observatories to study the stars.

whistle and even roar.

In some deserts around the world, there are sand dunes that produce haunting sounds – from whistles and barks, to deep rumbles and roars.

Scientists believe that the noises occur because the sand grains contain a mineral called **quartz**.

Here's how it happens:
Desert wind causes sand to cascade down the side of dunes. This makes the grains of sand rub together, so the quartz in them vibrates.

Grains of a similar rounded shape and size all vibrate at the same frequency – **about 100 times per second**.

When lots of sand grains vibrate together, they produce sounds loud enough to hear.

Different sizes of grain produce different musical notes.

Sand in Morocco –
0.15–0.17mm
(0.006–0.007 inches)

Note produced –
a low **G sharp**

Sand in Oman –
0.15–0.31mm
(0.006–0.012 inches)

Notes produced –
9 notes between **F sharp** and **D**

The sounds of singing sand can carry up to **15km (9 miles)**.

SHHHH!

15 Sand thieves...

are stealing entire beaches.

A new type of crime is damaging coastlines around the world. Gangs of sand thieves are digging up beaches, loading sand into trucks, and smuggling it away to building sites.

Each year, **tens of billions of truck loads** of sand are used to make concrete and glass to construct roads and buildings around the world.

Not just any sand will do. Grains of desert sand are too round and smooth for making concrete. Rougher sand from beaches and rivers is best.

But this sand is surprisingly scarce.

It takes thousands of years for rocks, shells and coral to be worn down into little grains, and then washed up on beaches by rivers and ocean tides.

People use sand in greater quantities than *any* other natural resource – apart from water.

Demand is so high that criminal gangs are now digging up whole beaches to sell to the highest bidder.

16 The world's biggest waterfall...

is an underwater waterfall.

The Angel Falls in Venezuela is the world's tallest waterfall on land. But under the sea, between Iceland and Greenland, there is a waterfall three times higher. It's called the **Denmark Strait cataract**.

People disagree over which waterfall on land is the *biggest*, because there are different ways of measuring them.

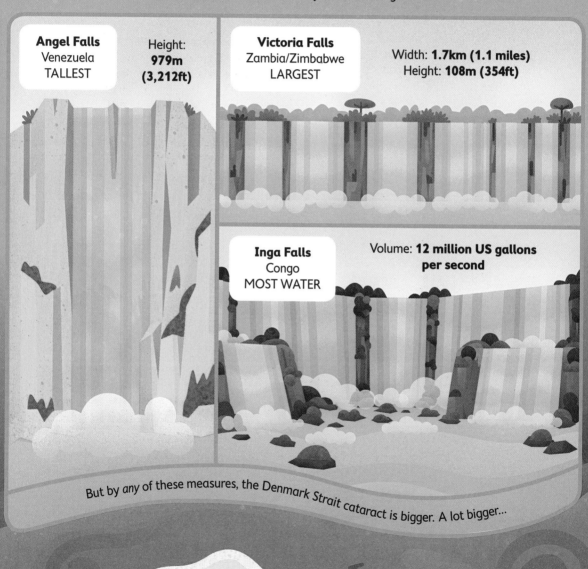

Angel Falls
Venezuela
TALLEST

Height:
979m
(3,212ft)

Victoria Falls
Zambia/Zimbabwe
LARGEST

Width: **1.7km (1.1 miles)**
Height: **108m (354ft)**

Inga Falls
Congo
MOST WATER

Volume: **12 million US gallons per second**

But by *any* of these measures, the Denmark Strait cataract is bigger. A lot bigger...

Landmass cross-section

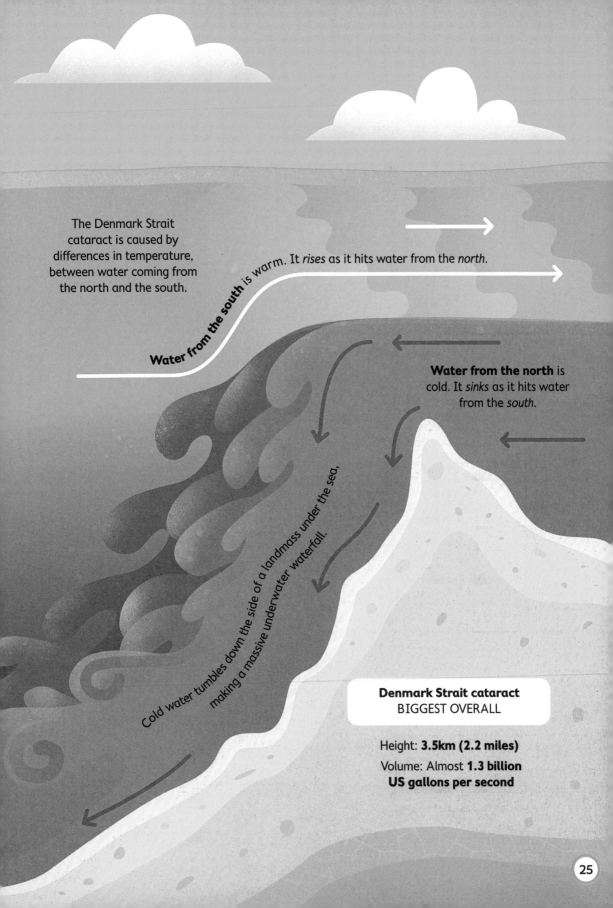

The Denmark Strait cataract is caused by differences in temperature, between water coming from the north and the south.

Water from the south is warm. It *rises* as it hits water from the *north*.

Water from the north is cold. It *sinks* as it hits water from the *south*.

Cold water tumbles down the side of a landmass under the sea, making a massive underwater waterfall.

Denmark Strait cataract
BIGGEST OVERALL

Height: **3.5km (2.2 miles)**
Volume: Almost **1.3 billion US gallons per second**

Astronomers of the future...

will see a different North Star.

The Earth spins around a north-south axis – an imaginary line through the planet. In the north, Earth's axis points to a star traditionally known as the North Star. But the North Star won't always be the *same* star...

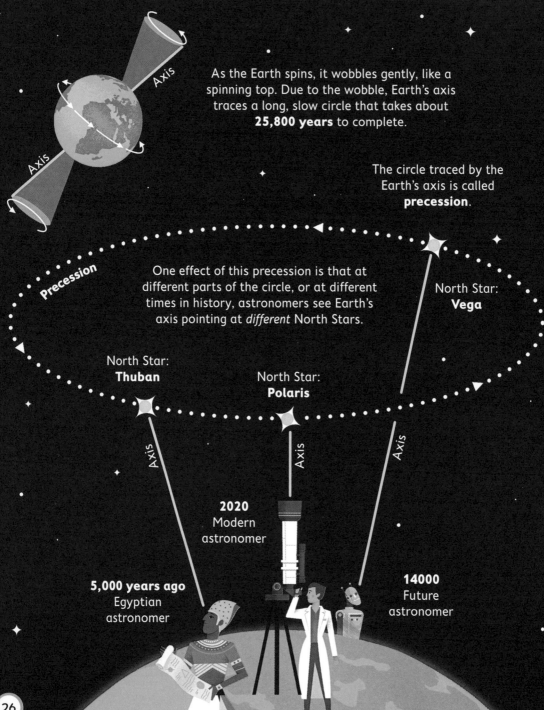

Axis

As the Earth spins, it wobbles gently, like a spinning top. Due to the wobble, Earth's axis traces a long, slow circle that takes about **25,800 years** to complete.

Axis

The circle traced by the Earth's axis is called **precession**.

Precession

One effect of this precession is that at different parts of the circle, or at different times in history, astronomers see Earth's axis pointing at *different* North Stars.

North Star:
Vega

North Star:
Thuban

North Star:
Polaris

Axis

Axis

Axis

2020
Modern
astronomer

5,000 years ago
Egyptian
astronomer

14000
Future
astronomer

18 Without the Moon...

the Earth would seesaw catastrophically.

Even if it *didn't* wobble (see page 26), the Earth wouldn't stand up straight on its axis. It is constantly leaning, or tilting, at an angle that slowly varies between 22.1 and 24.5 degrees. But *without* the steadying effects of the Moon, the Earth would seesaw dangerously back and forth...

With no Moon, Earth's tilt could vary by as much as 85 degrees – causing unstable climates...

Too hot...

Axis

...and plunging the planet into thousands of years of ice ages.

Axis

Brrrrrrr

Luckily, the Moon is big enough for its gravity to pull on Planet Earth. This keeps the Earth stable, so that the tilt of its axis changes by only 2.4 degrees.

I got you, buddy!

This effect is one of the things that makes life possible on Earth.

19 A creaking sinkhole...

is releasing poisonous gases.

In the freezing north east of Russia lies a huge sinkhole, or **megaslump**, called the Batagaika Crater. It emits gases and eerie noises, and is warm enough to melt ice. Locals nickname it *the doorway to the underworld*.

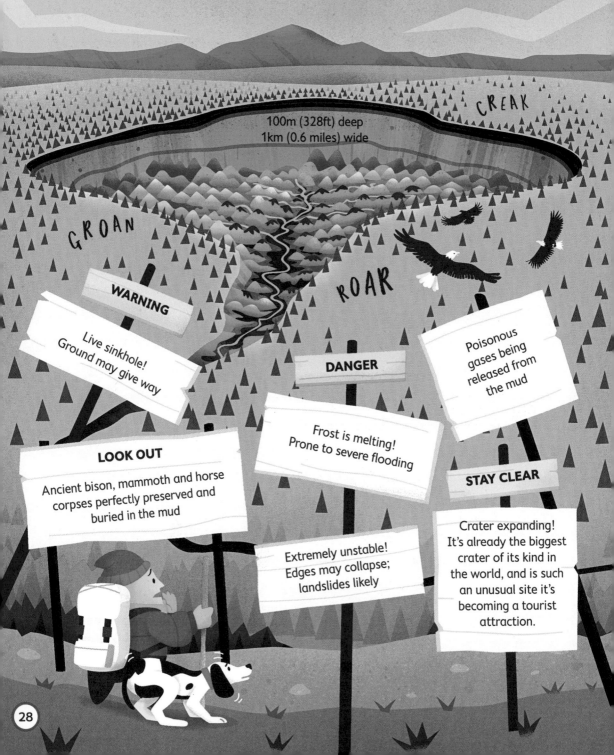

CREAK

100m (328ft) deep
1km (0.6 miles) wide

GROAN

ROAR

WARNING

Live sinkhole!
Ground may give way

DANGER

Poisonous gases being released from the mud

LOOK OUT

Ancient bison, mammoth and horse corpses perfectly preserved and buried in the mud

Frost is melting!
Prone to severe flooding

STAY CLEAR

Extremely unstable!
Edges may collapse;
landslides likely

Crater expanding!
It's already the biggest crater of its kind in the world, and is such an unusual site it's becoming a tourist attraction.

20 The conscience pile...

is built of guilt, remorse, and petrified wood.

In the US state of Arizona, just outside the Petrified Forest National Park, lies a pile of brightly patterned stones. These stones are petrified wood: the remains of ancient trees which have turned into fossils.

The National Park protects the remains of a forest that's about 210 million years old.

Some visitors steal fossils as souvenirs, but many later send them back — out of remorse or fear that they bring bad luck.

The Petrified Forest

Wish you were here!

DEAR RANGER,

PLEASE TAKE THIS ROCK BACK. I'VE HAD NOTHING BUT ROTTEN, LOUSY LUCK SINCE I SLIPPED IT INTO MY POCKET.

- ANONYMOUS

Dear Ranger,

I took these fossils from your park last summer. They are lovely, but they belong where scientists can study them and everyone can enjoy them. I'm sorry — please forgive me!

Sincerely,
A Rock Lover

Petrified wood: How, What, Why?!

This log was buried millions of years ago. Minerals slowly seeped into the ground and filled up the tiny hollows inside it, replacing the wood with a detailed stone fossil.

Bark

Tree rings

The conscience pile

Park rangers add returned fossils to what they call the conscience pile.

The pile serves as a reminder to all who see it: it's up to us to preserve our planet's natural wonders.

29

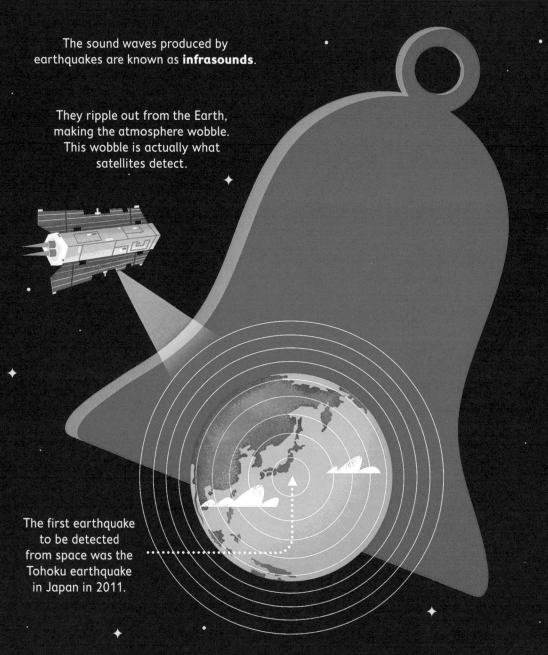

21 Massive earthquakes...

make the Earth ring like a bell.

When a powerful earthquake strikes, it makes the planet vibrate, sending sound waves out into the atmosphere. These are too low to be heard by human ears, but can be detected by satellites orbiting the Earth.

The sound waves produced by earthquakes are known as **infrasounds**.

They ripple out from the Earth, making the atmosphere wobble. This wobble is actually what satellites detect.

The first earthquake to be detected from space was the Tohoku earthquake in Japan in 2011.

Picking up infrasound waves allows scientists to pinpoint exactly where the earthquake originated, enabling emergency services to respond quickly to the places worst affected.

22 Plastiglomerate...

is rock made of junk.

In the last twenty years or so, a brand-new type of rock has begun to appear around the world. Called plastiglomerate, it is made of lumps of plastic debris that has melted, and mingled with sand, shells and pebbles.

Here are some more materials humans have made accidentally:

Trinitite...
is a mildly radioactive green glass formed from quartz and feldspar sand melted in the blast of a nuclear bomb test in 1945.

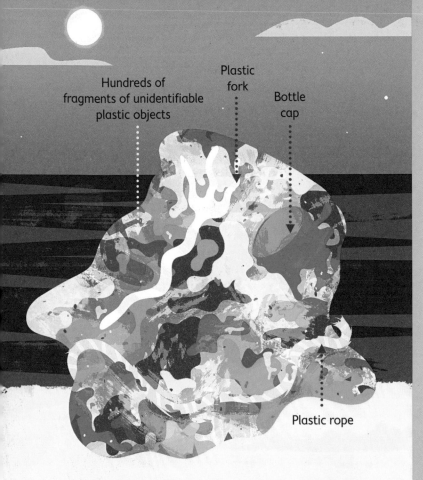

Hundreds of fragments of unidentifiable plastic objects

Plastic fork

Bottle cap

Plastic rope

Abhurite...
is a mineral formed by the exposure of tin to sea water. It is usually found inside shipwrecks containing cargoes of tin.

Plastiglomerate is usually formed when people build campfires on beaches heavily littered with plastic waste.

The heat of the campfires melts the plastic in the sand, creating gooey, rocky clods which could last for centuries.

War sand...
is sand mingled with tiny grains of iron, steel and glass. These are the remnants of bullets and bombs from a battle that took place in 1944 on the beaches of Normandy in France.

23 The Earth is a jigsaw puzzle...

that will never be completed.

The outer layer of the Earth is made up of vast sections, known as **tectonic plates**. These slot together like a giant jigsaw puzzle – except that the pieces don't have fixed positions...

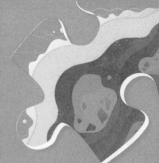

Tectonic plates constantly slide around very slowly, gradually arranging and rearranging continents and oceans.

Tectonic movement means that the Earth we know today will look very different **250 million years** from now.

By then, scientists predict the separate continents will probably have moved together to form a single supercontinent, known as **Pangea Proxima**.

24 A new ocean is forming...

in the middle of Africa.

The plates are still moving apart by a staggering 2.5cm (1in) every year.

In 2005, a huge crack started to open up between two tectonic plates in Ethiopia.

RED SEA

DABBAHU RIFT

GULF OF ADEN

The crack, known as the Dabbahu Rift, is 60km (37 miles) long and grew up to 8m (26ft) wide in just 3 weeks when it first opened up.

If the crack continues to grow, nearby seas will flood into it, forming a colossal new ocean.

BREAKING NEWS

STAY TUNED: SCIENTISTS THINK THIS NEW OCEAN COULD FORM IN THE NEXT 1 TO 10 MILLION YEARS.

25 The Earth is a giant magnet...

that defends us from certain death.

The Earth's core is surrounded by a swirling layer of liquid iron.
The movement of this layer creates a powerful **magnetic field**,
extending from pole to pole and out into space. It protects the
planet from the harmful effects of the Sun.

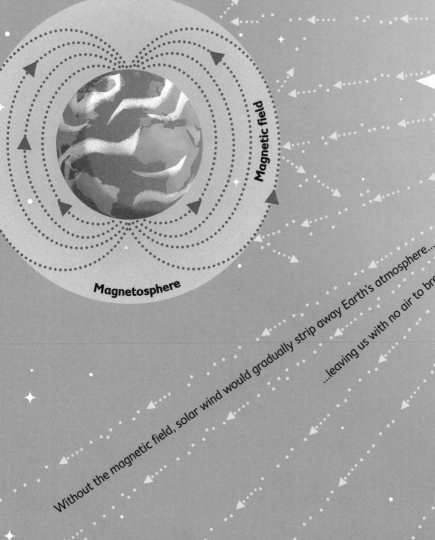

The Sun radiates deadly particles known as **solar wind**.

The magnetic field creates a barrier around
the planet known as the **magnetosphere**.
This deflects solar wind.

Magnetic field

Magnetosphere

Without the magnetic field, solar wind would gradually strip away Earth's atmosphere...

...leaving us with no air to breathe.

Seabird droppings...

help keep the Arctic cool.

Every summer in the Arctic, colonies of seabirds leave behind huge amounts of droppings. Scientists have found that a smelly chemical called ammonia, released from the droppings, has a vital cooling effect.

Millions of seabirds, such as fulmars, kittiwakes, guillemots and puffins, migrate to the Arctic to breed between May and September.

The seabirds eat lots of fish, which affects the chemical composition of their droppings.

Ammonia particle

Ammonia is released when their droppings break down.

These new particles clump together, forming bright, reflective clouds. The clouds reflect the Sun's rays back, helping to keep the Arctic cool.

Newly-formed particle

Ammonia reacts with chemicals in ocean spray to form new particles.

27 Gravity can be weaker...

in different parts of the world.

Gravity is the force that keeps our feet on Earth – but its strength isn't the same everywhere. Studies show that the Hudson Bay area of Canada has weaker gravity than the rest of the country. Here's how:

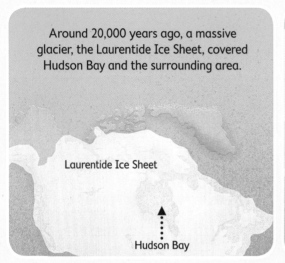

Around 20,000 years ago, a massive glacier, the Laurentide Ice Sheet, covered Hudson Bay and the surrounding area.

Laurentide Ice Sheet

Hudson Bay

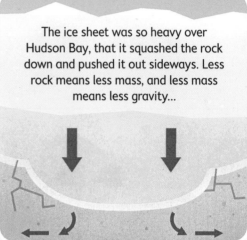

The ice sheet was so heavy over Hudson Bay, that it squashed the rock down and pushed it out sideways. Less rock means less mass, and less mass means less gravity...

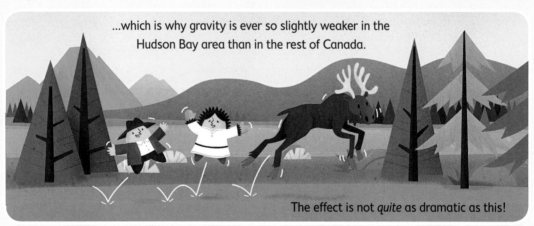

...which is why gravity is ever so slightly weaker in the Hudson Bay area than in the rest of Canada.

The effect is not *quite* as dramatic as this!

The rock is slowly building back up, and over the next 5,000 years, the gravity there will gradually grow stronger too.

28 Rain as red as blood...

once fell in India.

From July to September 2001, red drops fell in the southern Indian state of Kerala. The streets flooded with red water and hanging laundry was stained red. Scientists disagree about what caused this, but over time they have built a clearer picture...

July 2001

I think it was an exploding meteor that scattered red dust.

November 2001

I disagree. Under a microscope, I can see **spores** in the rain — tiny particles that grow to become plant-like organisms called algae.

2003

I think the red spores may have arrived from another planet — it's a sign that aliens exist.

2015

Pah! No way. The red algae spores in the rain are the same species as one found in Austria.

The most convincing explanation is that red algae spores blew all the way from somewhere in Europe to Kerala, then fell as rain.

29 We live in the 99th age...

of the 34th epoch, 12th period, 3rd era in the 4th eon.

Earth is a little over **4.5 billion** years old. To make sense of such a vast span of time, geologists have divided it into units called **eons**. The first three eons lasted over 1 billion years each. The current, fourth eon, is subdivided into 3 **eras**, 12 **periods**, 34 **epochs** and, so far, 99 **ages**.

30 Vulcan Point was an island...
in a lake... on an island... in a lake... on an island.

Vulcan Point was a small island in the middle of a lake, called Main Crater Lake, which formed on Volcano Island after a volcanic eruption in 1911.

Both Vulcan Point and Main Crater Lake disappeared again, after another volcanic eruption in 2020.

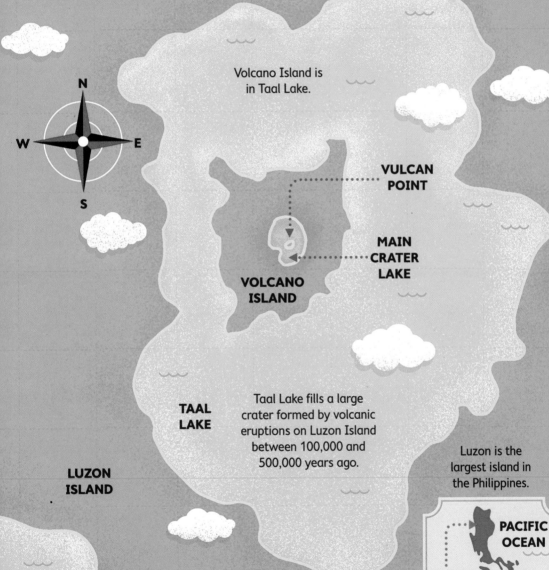

Volcano Island is in Taal Lake.

N

W   E

S

VULCAN POINT

MAIN CRATER LAKE

VOLCANO ISLAND

Taal Lake fills a large crater formed by volcanic eruptions on Luzon Island between 100,000 and 500,000 years ago.

TAAL LAKE

Luzon is the largest island in the Philippines.

LUZON ISLAND

PACIFIC OCEAN

PACIFIC OCEAN

LUZON

The Philippines

There's a rare kind of lightning...

that looks like jellyfish.

Most thunderstorms happen when tiny particles of ice in clouds rub together. This creates friction, which makes static electricity that can cause lightning. But there's a rare type of lightning, known as jellyfish sprites, that doesn't seem to fit the usual pattern...

In 1989, cameras on board a space shuttle filmed gigantic flashes of orange-red lightning high above thunder clouds. These were named **jellyfish sprites,** because of their shape.

Scientists are still investigating exactly what causes the sprites. They occur high *above* storm clouds, unlike most lightning which forms *within* clouds.

Sprites only occur very rarely. This makes them difficult for scientists to study.

Bright red bell shapes

Tendrils hanging down below

Jellyfish sprites can be almost **50km (31 miles)** tall and wide.

Some unexpected conditions can create thunder and lightning. Below are some examples.

Firestorms

Forest fires make huge ash clouds. The specks of ash sometimes rub together and make lightning.

Firestorm strikes are especially dangerous as they may start even more fires.

Thundersnowstorms

Thunderstorms in winter are rare, but they can be created by snowflakes swirling in the clouds during blizzards.

The explosions can also make it rain.

Nuclear lightning

Nuclear explosions create huge changes in air pressure, which sometimes create lightning.

Dirty thunderstorms

In dirty thunderstorms, the ash and dust spewed out of a volcano can rub together to make lightning.

32 A hole in the atmosphere...

can heal itself.

Earth is surrounded by a shield of gas called the **ozone layer**, that protects the planet from the Sun's hot rays. Over Antarctica, there's a hole where the layer has been damaged by chemical pollution, but that damage can be undone.

The hole was discovered in the **1980s**. Human use of chemicals, particularly a kind known as CFCs used in spray cans, was making this hole grow at an alarming rate.

In **1989** there was a worldwide ban on CFCs, in an attempt to stop the hole from getting bigger. Records have shown that as CFCs disappeared from the atmosphere, the ozone layer started to thicken up — literally healing itself.

The CFC ban is considered the most effective piece of environmental regulation so far. But it is vital that people work together to make sure the hole is able to shrink.

33 Seemingly lifeless glaciers...

are actually teeming with tiny creatures.

Glaciers are bleak, frozen, apparently lifeless places. But in fact, thousands of microscopic creatures find a haven there inside **glacier mice**: mouse-sized, fuzzy clumps of moss that tumble in the wind across the icy wastes.

To their residents, these moist, spongy balls are like tiny luxury hotels.

It's 0°C (32°F) out here – it's literally freezing!

Well, it's a balmy **2-10°C (36-50°F)** in here!

They offer food...

...water...

Pebble

...and shelter from the wind and cold.

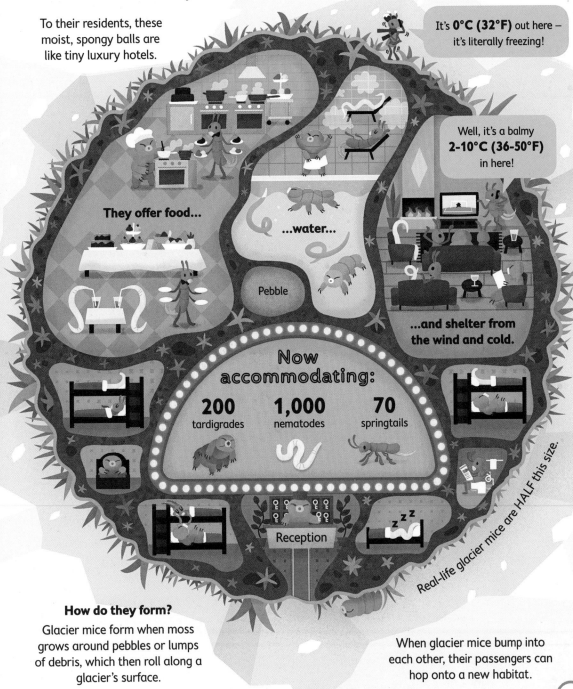

Now accommodating:

200 tardigrades

1,000 nematodes

70 springtails

Reception

Real-life glacier mice are HALF this size.

How do they form?

Glacier mice form when moss grows around pebbles or lumps of debris, which then roll along a glacier's surface.

When glacier mice bump into each other, their passengers can hop onto a new habitat.

34 You'll need to change your look...

to suit Earth's changing climate.

When oil and coal are burned, they produce carbon dioxide – a gas that causes the atmosphere to trap heat. As a result, scientists predict that average global temperatures could rise by **2–8°C (36–46°F)** over the next 100 years. What could this mean for us? Nothing good...

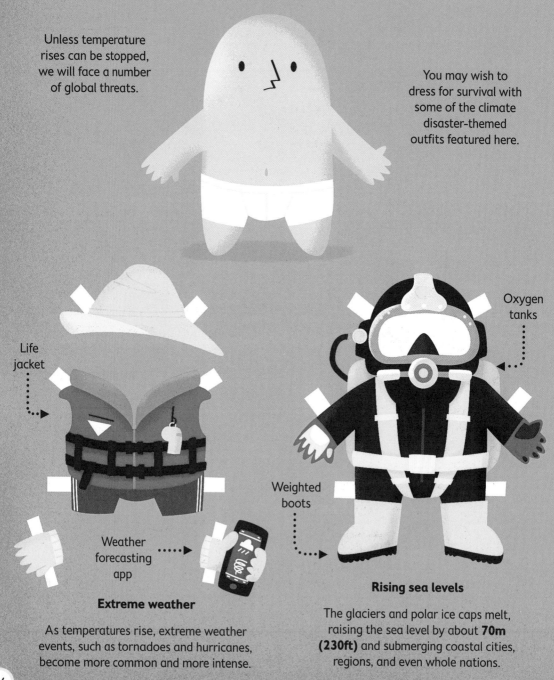

Unless temperature rises can be stopped, we will face a number of global threats.

You may wish to dress for survival with some of the climate disaster-themed outfits featured here.

Life jacket

Oxygen tanks

Weighted boots

Weather forecasting app

Extreme weather

As temperatures rise, extreme weather events, such as tornadoes and hurricanes, become more common and more intense.

Rising sea levels

The glaciers and polar ice caps melt, raising the sea level by about **70m (230ft)** and submerging coastal cities, regions, and even whole nations.

Checklist for tallying lost species

Plague bacteria

Air filter

Waders

Ancient diseases

Viruses and bacteria that cause diseases such as smallpox and the bubonic plague have long been frozen in the polar ice. Now they melt into the water system, infecting people on a global scale.

Acidic oceans

The oceans absorb carbon dioxide gas, which makes the water more and more acidic. Fish and corals die, leaving behind a watery wasteland.

Dust goggles

Hydration system

Nuclear launch codes

Combat medals

Droughts and dust bowls

Massive droughts become commonplace. Earth's currently fertile regions become too hot to grow crops efficiently. Forests and farmland turn to dust. Food is scarce.

Brand new wars

International quarrels about dwindling food supplies, access to fresh water and farmland lead to global warfare.

35 Boulders are bigger...

than cobbles... and cobbles are bigger than pebbles...

To geologists, a lump of rock is never just a *lump*. They use a precise scale called the **Udden-Wentworth Scale** to determine the difference between boulders, cobbles and pebbles – right down to the tiniest granules.

Here's how it works.

Boulder
Size range: anything bigger than 256mm (10.1in)

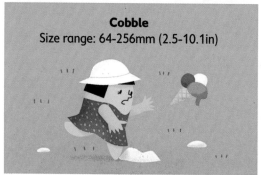

Cobble
Size range: 64-256mm (2.5-10.1in)

Pebble
Size range: 4-64mm (0.16-2.5in)

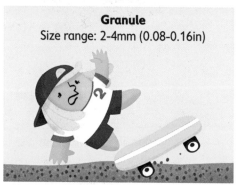

Granule
Size range: 2-4mm (0.08-0.16in)

Sand
Size range: 0.06mm-2mm (0.002-0.08in)

Grains smaller than sand are hard to see but are still classified...

...into **silt**...

...and **clay**.

Silt particles are miniscule, but clay particles are even smaller.

36 Graffiti...

could save a species.

Every year, thousands of endangered animals are traded illegally – sold as pets or for valuable body parts. To save some species, such as the rare ploughshare tortoise, conservationists are resorting to extreme measures.

Ploughshare tortoises have beautiful black and gold shells, which make them attractive to some people who buy them as exotic pets.

As a result of this illegal trade, these tortoises are critically endangered – there are fewer than 100 left in the wild.

Spraying graffiti on their shells makes them much less valuable.

Similar measures are taken to protect rhinos. Illegal poachers hunt rhinos to sell their horns, so some conservationists safely remove horns, making the animals worthless to poachers.

These approaches are controversial, as it's not clear whether or not they harm the animals. But there is evidence that it reduces illegal trade in those species, so most people think it's worth a try.

37 The driest place on Earth...

is in Antarctica.

Amid the snow and ice of western Antarctica lies a row of dry, wind-swept valleys called the McMurdo Dry Valleys. They are drier than any other place on Earth – drier even than the Atacama Desert in Chile.*

This year, why not visit...

The McMurdo Dry Valleys

Dry, warm and ice-free, thanks to glacier-blocking peaks and **katabatic winds!**

Katabatic winds form when cold air flows down a mountainside, pulled by gravity. It gets warmer as it descends, and makes water, snow and ice evaporate.

Tired of traffic? The Dry Valleys have **no roads!**

* See page 20.

38 When islands form...
new wildlife gradually develops.

Some islands are formed when an area of land becomes permanently cut off from the mainland. Over millions of years, the plants and animals on the island and the mainland develop distinct characteristics. As a result, many islands have plants and animals that aren't found anywhere else.

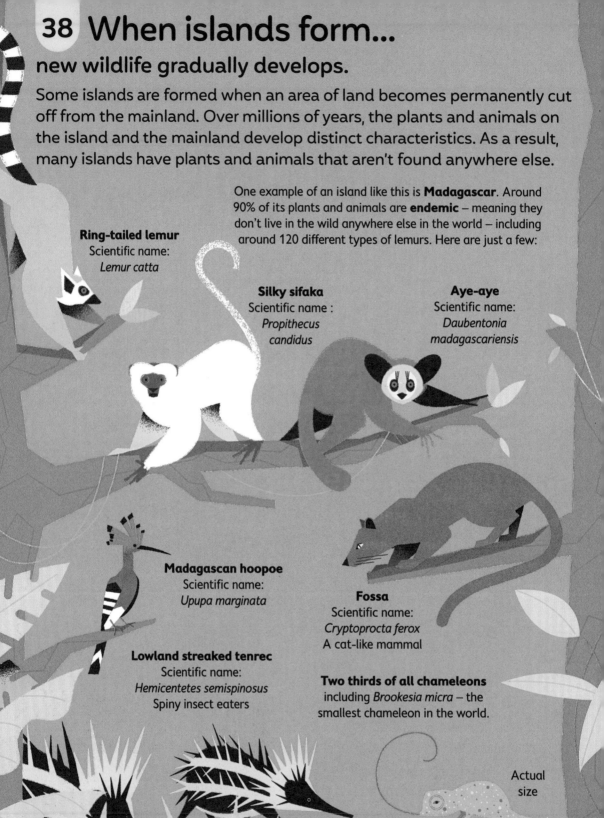

One example of an island like this is **Madagascar**. Around 90% of its plants and animals are **endemic** – meaning they don't live in the wild anywhere else in the world – including around 120 different types of lemurs. Here are just a few:

Ring-tailed lemur
Scientific name:
Lemur catta

Silky sifaka
Scientific name :
Propithecus candidus

Aye-aye
Scientific name:
Daubentonia madagascariensis

Madagascan hoopoe
Scientific name:
Upupa marginata

Fossa
Scientific name:
Cryptoprocta ferox
A cat-like mammal

Lowland streaked tenrec
Scientific name:
Hemicentetes semispinosus
Spiny insect eaters

Two thirds of all chameleons
including *Brookesia micra* – the smallest chameleon in the world.

Actual size

39 Every tree on Earth...

recorded the invention of nuclear bombs.

The first nuclear weapon was detonated in 1945. In the years that followed, scientists around the world raced to develop – and test – newer, bigger and deadlier nuclear bombs. Their efforts altered every living tree on the planet.

In the 1950s and 60s, hundreds of nuclear bombs were tested around the world – most in the open air.

The tests released floods of tiny particles called **neutrinos** that reacted with Earth's atmosphere, producing a dramatic increase in a rare type of carbon atom: **carbon-14**.

This carbon-14 spread around the world.

Trees everywhere absorbed it from the atmosphere,

and it was stored in their trunks.

After nuclear bombs

Before nuclear bombs

The carbon-14 in tree trunks can't be seen with the naked eye – but if scientists test the wood from trees that were alive in the 1950s, they detect a sudden leap in carbon-14 levels.

Nuclear testing has become less frequent, and carbon-14 levels are slowly falling.

Carbon-14 level

| 1930 | 1940 | 1950 | 1960 | 1970 | 1980 |

40 A pack of wolves...

changed the course of a river.

To protect their farms and livestock, human hunters drove wolves out of Yellowstone National Park, in the US. This had unexpected effects not only on the wildlife in the park, but also on the landscape itself.

Yellowstone, 1926

Without wolves hunting them, the elk population exploded.

Aspen tree

Lamar River

As so many elk were grazing on them, aspen trees began to disappear.

The river banks started to collapse because there were no longer enough tree roots there to hold the soil together.

This made the river flow faster and become more winding.

Yellowstone, 1995

Elk numbers had soared to around 20,000.

Young aspen were rarely surviving to become fully grown trees.

Conservationists reintroduced a pack of wolves back into the park.

AWOOOOOOO

The wolves began to hunt the elk.

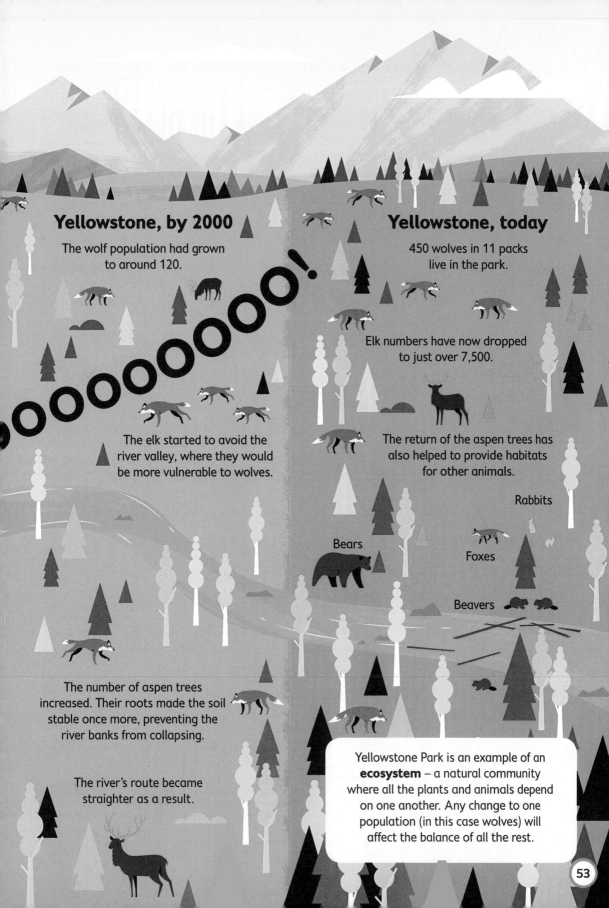

Yellowstone, by 2000

The wolf population had grown to around 120.

The elk started to avoid the river valley, where they would be more vulnerable to wolves.

The number of aspen trees increased. Their roots made the soil stable once more, preventing the river banks from collapsing.

The river's route became straighter as a result.

OOOOOOOOO!

Yellowstone, today

450 wolves in 11 packs live in the park.

Elk numbers have now dropped to just over 7,500.

The return of the aspen trees has also helped to provide habitats for other animals.

Rabbits

Bears

Foxes

Beavers

Yellowstone Park is an example of an **ecosystem** – a natural community where all the plants and animals depend on one another. Any change to one population (in this case wolves) will affect the balance of all the rest.

41 When valleys talk...
submarines listen.

SILENCE

Hello? Hello?

Normal radio waves can't reach very far through seawater, so once a submarine is submerged, it becomes cut off from most communication.

But in the 1950s, engineers had a bright idea.

Radio waves that can reach underwater!

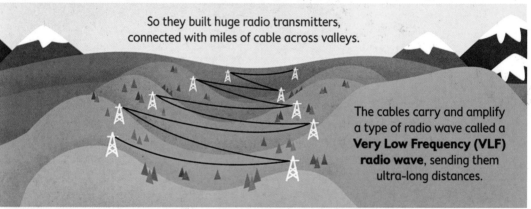

So they built huge radio transmitters, connected with miles of cable across valleys.

The cables carry and amplify a type of radio wave called a **Very Low Frequency (VLF) radio wave**, sending them ultra-long distances.

These VLF waves bounce in a zigzag inside the atmosphere, right around the Earth.

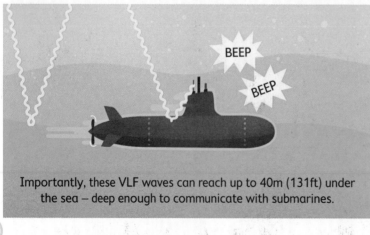

BEEP

BEEP

Importantly, these VLF waves can reach up to 40m (131ft) under the sea – deep enough to communicate with submarines.

Receiving loud and clear!

42 An accidental bubble...

helps to keep the Earth safe.

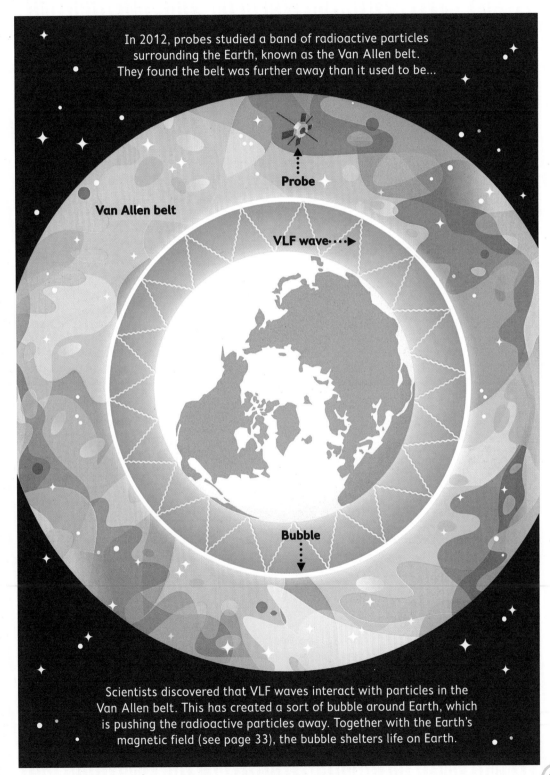

In 2012, probes studied a band of radioactive particles
surrounding the Earth, known as the Van Allen belt.
They found the belt was further away than it used to be...

Probe

Van Allen belt

VLF wave····▶

Bubble

Scientists discovered that VLF waves interact with particles in the
Van Allen belt. This has created a sort of bubble around Earth, which
is pushing the radioactive particles away. Together with the Earth's
magnetic field (see page 33), the bubble shelters life on Earth.

43 Zastrugi, firn and frazil...

are all types of snow and ice.

Snow and ice are made of nothing more than frozen water, but variables such as sun, wind, temperature and pressure give them countless different forms and properties – each with their own, often beautiful, name.

This crossword puzzle is composed entirely of terms used to describe snow and ice. Match up each one to its definition.

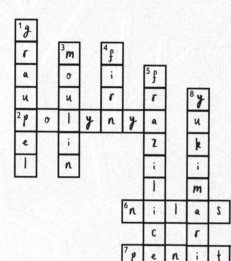

Across:

2. A naturally formed area of open water surrounded by floating sea ice (7)
6. A flexible crust of sea ice up to 10cm (4in) thick (5)
7. A high-altitude snow formation of closely packed blades or spires (10)
9. Underwater ice attached to a sea floor or lake bed, for example (6, 3)
12. A tower of ice, found in a glacier where crevasses intersect (5)
14. A compact layer of windblown snow found in a sheltered space (4, 4)

Down:

1. Pellets formed when supercooled water freezes on falling snowflakes (7)
3. A steeply sloping chute in a glacier, through which liquid water flows (6)
4. Granular snow more than one year old, not yet compacted into ice (4)
5. A slushy suspension of randomly shaped ice crystals in water (6, 3)
8. Balls of frost that roll like tumbleweeds across Antarctica (10)
10. An overhanging ledge formed by windblown snow, especially along a mountain ridge (7)
11. Wind-worn shapes in hard snow (8)
13. A mass of layered sheets of ice (6)

The remotest place on Earth...

is closer to space than it is to dry land.

The remotest place on Earth is the **pole of inaccessibility** in the Pacific Ocean.

PACIFIC OCEAN

Nicknamed **Point Nemo**, the pole is the farthest point from dry land on the planet.

POINT
✕
NEMO

SOUTH AMERICA

Space officially begins **100km (62 miles)** above the Earth, while the nearest dry land to Point Nemo is **2,688km (1,670 miles)** away.

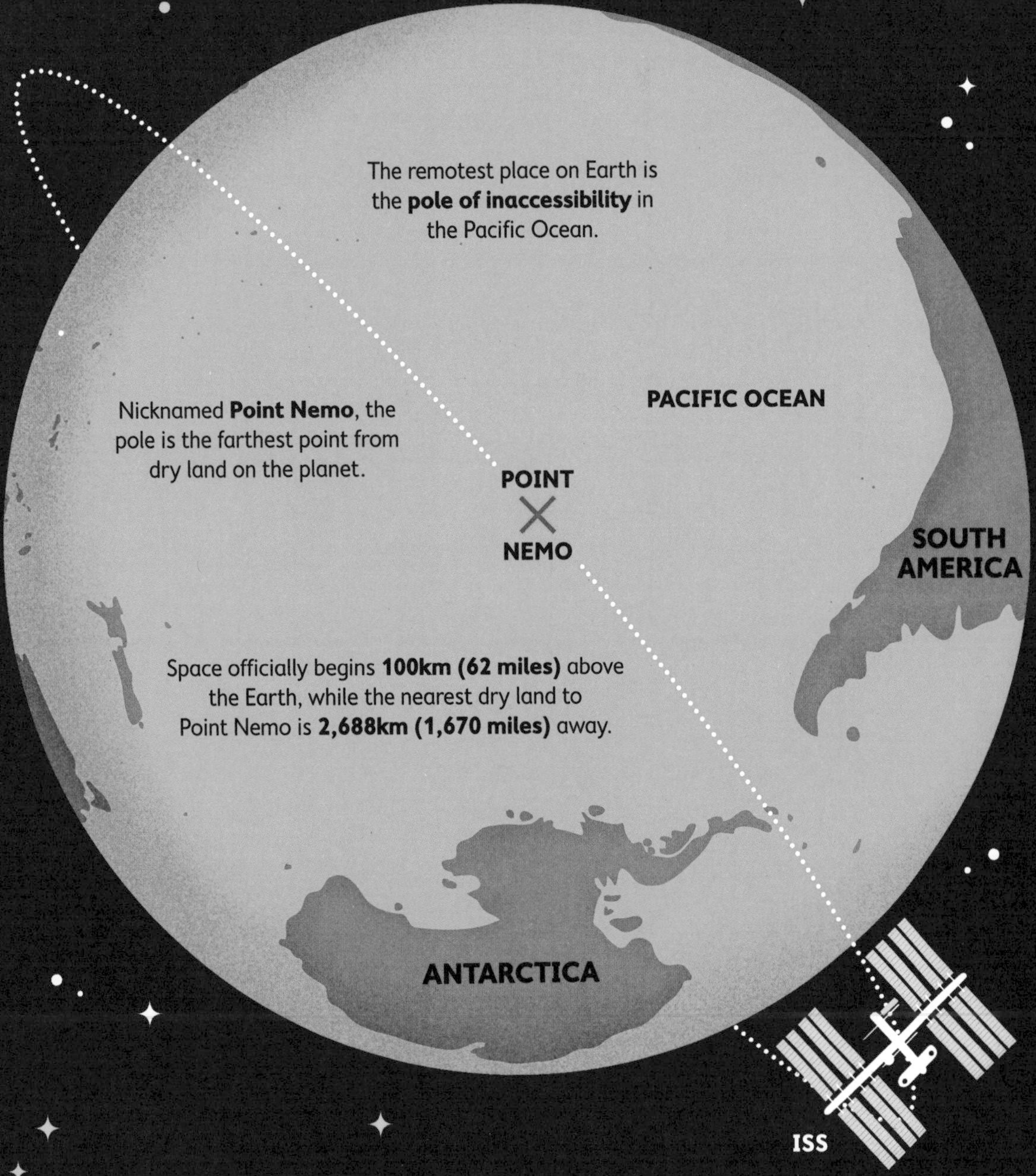

ANTARCTICA

ISS

Often, the people closest to Point Nemo are the astronauts aboard the International Space Station (ISS) as it passes **408km (254 miles)** directly overhead, 16 times a day.

45 1,600 balloons a day...

help weather forecasters get it right.

Measuring the weather is best done from high up in the air. Around the world, in 800 different locations, meteorologists launch new weather balloons *every 12 hours* to track – and help forecast – changing conditions.

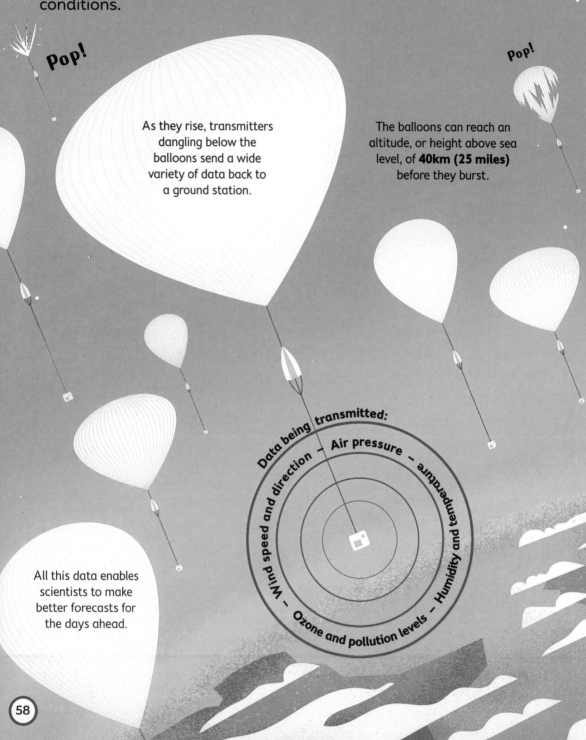

Pop!

As they rise, transmitters dangling below the balloons send a wide variety of data back to a ground station.

The balloons can reach an altitude, or height above sea level, of **40km (25 miles)** before they burst.

Pop!

Data being transmitted:

Wind speed and direction – Air pressure – Humidity and temperature – Ozone and pollution levels –

All this data enables scientists to make better forecasts for the days ahead.

46 Tsunami stones...

remind us of disasters yet to come.

Throughout history, Japan has been hit by **tsunamis**: huge ocean waves usually triggered by earthquakes. Carved monuments called **tsunami stones** line the coast as memorials – and to warn future generations.

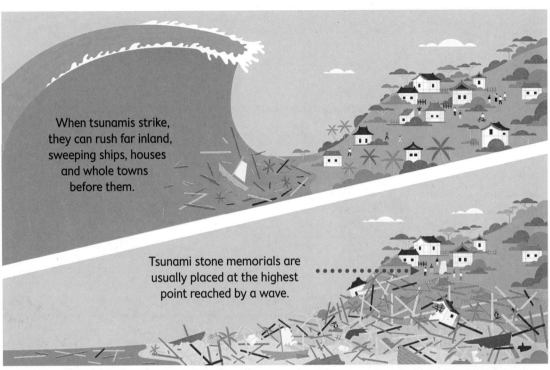

When tsunamis strike, they can rush far inland, sweeping ships, houses and whole towns before them.

Tsunami stone memorials are usually placed at the highest point reached by a wave.

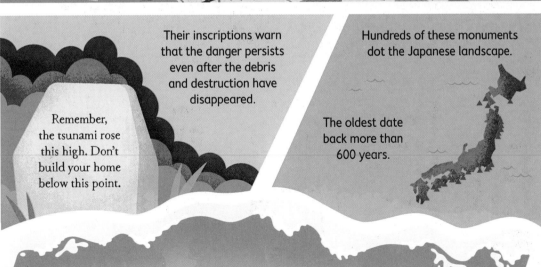

Their inscriptions warn that the danger persists even after the debris and destruction have disappeared.

Remember, the tsunami rose this high. Don't build your home below this point.

Hundreds of these monuments dot the Japanese landscape.

The oldest date back more than 600 years.

Tsunamis are still a threat – but in Japan, early warning systems using ocean buoys and satellites are now in place. Along with the tsunami stones, these will help save more lives.

47 Arctic foxes...

are excellent gardeners.

On treeless plains near the Arctic Circle, where the ground is always frozen, little grows. But, scattered across this barren landscape, are little gardens full of life. Each marks the location of an Arctic fox den.

The ground near these underground fox dens is rich in nutrients from their droppings, urine, and the remains of their prey.

These nutrients support many species of plants, and the dens attract grazing animals and scavengers from all around.

Arctic foxes usually have six to ten cubs each year.

Much of the Arctic is made up of permafrost – frozen ground that never thaws.

It takes lots of energy to dig a new den, so foxes often use existing sites — sometimes stealing them from other animals, such as ground squirrels.

A den can be occupied for more than 100 years, and foxes continue to maintain their gardens for generation after generation.

TOILET

Wayside Lodge
Built by ground squirrels in 1910

South-facing entrance to catch sunlight

Bird eggs

Foxes store food to eat in the winter.

Arctic fox dens feature a maze of tunnels to confuse any predators.

Arctic foxes change their coats for winter.

Seaweed   Insects   Berries

In their thick winter coats, they don't shiver unless the temperature drops below **-70°C (-94°F)**.

Pure white for camouflage in snow

Lemming

Goose

Vole

48 Antarctica was covered in forest...

100 million years ago.

Today, Antarctica is covered in ice, but fossils show that 100 million years ago it was a lush forest. Trees need sunlight to grow, but the region is completely dark for many months of the year, so scientists are interested in how these forests survived.

Plants use sunlight to create the energy they need to survive – a process called **photosynthesis**. But during the dark winter months the Antarctic forests would have been starved of light.

Antarctica, 100 million years ago

49 Antarctica froze...

after the Himalayan mountains rose.

About **34 million years ago**, the tectonic plates forming Earth's outer layers collided under southern Asia. As a result, the Himalayan mountains rose up, with surprising consequences...

Southern Asia, 34 million years ago

Plates pushed against each other, forcing the **Himalayan mountains** further upwards.

Lots more rock became exposed to wind and rain. All this additional rock absorbed carbon dioxide from the atmosphere...

Moving plates

Scientists think the trees made huge stores of energy in the summer, when the Sun shines 24 hours a day.

These stores kept the plants alive during the dark winter months.

Carbon dioxide (CO_2) in the air traps heat inside Earth's atmosphere.

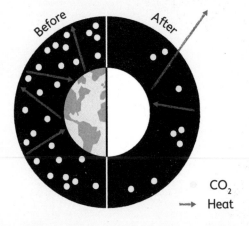

Before

After

CO_2

→ Heat

With more CO_2 absorbed by the rock and less in the atmosphere, more heat was able to escape. Scientists think it could be as a result of this, that the planet cooled by 8°C (46°F) and entered an ice age.

During the cold snap Antarctica froze over, and it has been covered in a permanent ice sheet ever since.

BRR

13,000km (8,000 miles) from the Himalayas

Antarctica, today

50 Diamonds travel...

at supersonic speeds.

Diamonds are formed deep underground – at least 150km (93 miles) beneath the Earth's surface. So how do they make their way up to where they can be mined?

The answer is that the diamonds hitch a supersonic ride on a type of eruption called a **volcanic pipe**.

Earth's crust

Earth's mantle

2

A volcanic pipe occurs when molten rock, or **magma**, erupts straight up through the mantle and crust. (This type of eruption is extremely rare.)

1

Diamonds are created when carbon is compressed in the high pressure and heat of Earth's mantle – the deep layer of rock beneath the planet's crust.

3

Diamonds are carried along in the flow of the molten rock.

Despite the rock-melting heat, the diamonds don't just burn up underground. There's not enough oxygen here for a fire to start.

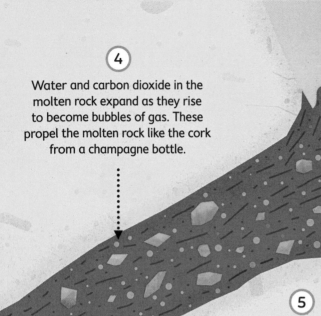

4

Water and carbon dioxide in the molten rock expand as they rise to become bubbles of gas. These propel the molten rock like the cork from a champagne bottle.

6

After the eruption, the molten rock cools to form a type of rock called **kimberlite**, which can be mined for the diamonds that have come up from below.

5

As it nears the surface, the eruption reaches supersonic speed – moving faster than the speed of sound.

51 A town made of diamonds...
rests in the crater where they were made.

Anyone taking a close look at the medieval walls of the German town of Nördlingen will find that the stones are speckled with millions of glittering, microscopic diamonds.

15 million years ago
An enormous asteroid struck, and the pressure and heat of impact crushed rocks, turning the carbon they contained into microscopic diamonds.

Nördlingen today
St. Georg's Church contains about 5,000 carats – roughly **1kg (2.2lb)** – of diamond.

The asteroid left behind a crater 24km (15 miles) across – and the diamond-studded rock that was later used to build Nördlingen.

entire planets were born.

1

Around 4.6 billion years ago, the Solar System consisted of the newly born Sun, surrounded by a swirling disc of cosmic dust known as an **accretion disc**.

2

As the microscopic dust particles in the accretion disc orbited the Sun, they bumped into each other.

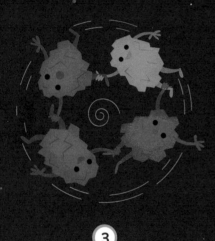

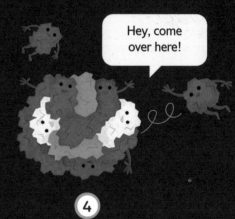

Hey, come over here!

3

When they bumped into each other, some dust particles stuck together and started to spin.

4

Slowly, they attracted more cosmic dust, forming a clump that grew bigger and bigger.

5

Over millions of years, one such clump went on to form the Earth, spinning on its axis as it orbits the Sun. The same process created the other planets in the solar system.

Mercury Venus Earth Mars Jupiter Saturn Uranus Neptune

Earth
was formed around
4.54 billion years ago.

NWA 11119
is a grapefruit-sized
meteorite discovered
in a sand dune in
Mauritania in 2016.
It was formed around
4.56 billion years ago.

When NWA 11119 was formed,
what would later become the solar system's
four rocky inner planets – including Earth –
was still just swirls of cosmic
dust around the Sun.

Sun

Mercury

Venus

Earth

Mars

54 Burning Mountain...

has been blazing for 6,000 years.

Mount Wingen, Australia, is often called Burning Mountain – for a very good reason. A layer of coal has been burning beneath its rocky slopes for thousands of years.

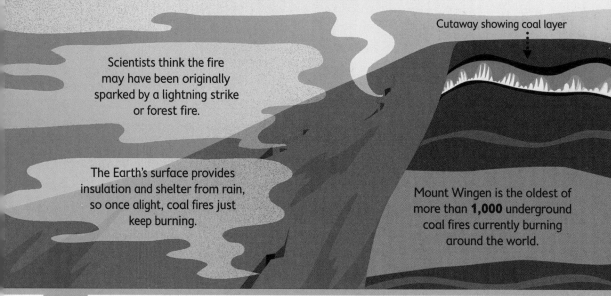

Cutaway showing coal layer

Scientists think the fire may have been originally sparked by a lightning strike or forest fire.

The Earth's surface provides insulation and shelter from rain, so once alight, coal fires just keep burning.

Mount Wingen is the oldest of more than **1,000** underground coal fires currently burning around the world.

55 Surfing the Pororoca...

can carry you miles inland.

The Guamá river in Brazil flows into the Atlantic Ocean – most of the time. But, at least twice a month, strong tides force a wave to travel in the opposite direction. This phenomenon is known locally as **Pororoca**, and scientists call it a **tidal bore**.

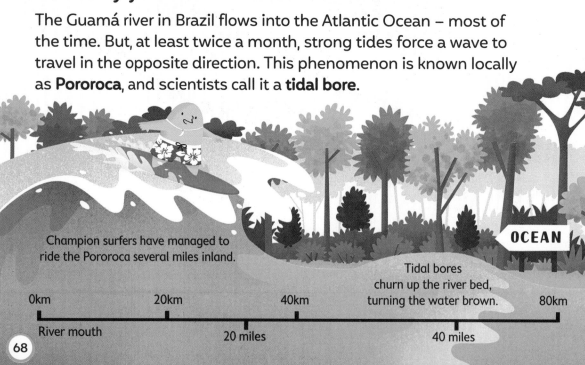

OCEAN

Champion surfers have managed to ride the Pororoca several miles inland.

Tidal bores churn up the river bed, turning the water brown.

0km	20km	40km	80km

River mouth

20 miles

40 miles

56 Underground goblins...

poisoned miners.

In the 16th century, miners digging for rocks containing copper under the Ore Mountains in Central Europe, started to hallucinate and become unwell. They thought they had been poisoned by evil goblins, called **kobolds**, living in the rocks. The rock became known as kobold too.

In fact, what was happening was that fumes of a toxic chemical called **arsenic** were being released, as miners dug.

Later, when they melted down the rocks to extract copper, an even more poisonous chemical was produced – **arsenic oxide**.

Much later, in the 18th century, a Swedish scientist discovered that the rock contained another substance, one nobody had seen before. He named it cobalt, from the German word *kobold*.

57 Arlene...

is the most common storm name.

Tropical storms are given internationally recognized names, to enable clear reporting and to aid an emergency response. But choosing names has always been complicated...

Abigail

Bruce

Charlotte

Elaine

Different regions choose their own lists of names. Each year a different list is written, with one name for each letter of the alphabet.

For many years, all storms were given female names.

Cerys

Debbie

Daniel

Agatha

Ellie

In 1975 **David** and **Cecil** became the first official hurricanes with male names. Lists today alternate male and female names.

David

Frank

Cecil

Some names are banned in certain regions. **Sonamu** was tried in Malaysia, but caused widespread panic, as it sounds too much like *tsunami*.

Sonamu

The names Charles and Diana were used for two storms in February 1978. Those names are no longer allowed, since Prince **Charles** married Lady **Diana** Spencer in 1981.

NEWSPAPER

STORM ARLENE HITS...

Diana

Charles

Arlene

The name **Arlene** has been use for 11 tropical storms since 1959.

Initially all storm names were very European, but today regions use names that reflect local names and languages.

58 A Venezuelan thunderstorm...

helps sailors find their way.

For centuries, sailors nearing the coast of Venezuela have been guided by the **Lighthouse of Maracaibo**. This is the name of a storm that always forms in the same spot and is visible up to 400km (250 miles) away.

Near the coast of Venezuela, above a lake called Maracaibo, clouds build high into the air.

At night, hemmed in by mountains, heat and moisture rise above the lake and often trigger huge storms.

Storm frequency:

Storm duration:

Average number of lightning flashes:

Maximum number of lightning flashes:

140-160
nights per year

up to
1,600,000
in one year

roughly **7-10**
hours at a time

280
per hour

up to **20,000**
in one night

59 Terns travel so far in their lives...

they could fly to the Moon and back three times.

Every year, Planet Earth is criss-crossed by the paths of hundreds of species as they embark on **migrations**. These will take them miles and miles across land and sea, to find food, warmth or places to breed.

Each year, terns fly at least **30,000km (18,600 miles)** south, and then even further on their way back again. Across their 30-year lives, it adds up to a distance equivalent to three trips to the Moon and back.

Siberian cranes can fly **320km (200 miles)** every day on their migration, soaring on currents of warm air.

Siberian crane

Every year 1.5 million wildebeest migrate **3,000km (1,900 miles)** around the Serengeti plain, to find fresh grass and water.

Wildebeest

Dragonfly

Arctic tern

Dragonflies migrate from India to Africa, following seasonal rains. It's such a long journey it takes longer than the lifetime of a single dragonfly – it takes four generations to complete the migration.

Journeys by sky

Journeys on land

Journeys by sea

Caribou migrate between Alaska and Canada to find enough food to put on body fat to survive winter.

Bar-tailed godwits undertake the longest journey without stopping, flying up to **11,000km (6,800 miles)**.

Caribou

More than 100 million butterflies fly **4,500km (2,800 miles)** south over North America for a warm winter.

Bar-tailed godwit

Monarch butterfly

Leatherback turtle

Leatherback turtles swim hundreds of miles to get from where they feed to where they lay eggs.

Humpback whale

Humpback whales migrate an average of **5,000km (3,100 miles)**, between warm breeding water and cold feeding water.

Adelie penguins follow the Sun, swimming around the edge of Antarctica, staying in sunlight as much as they can.

Adelie penguin

60 The Boring Billion...

was a billion years of nothing.

Between 1.8 and 0.8 billion years ago, Earth experienced a billion years of total stability. One scientist termed this time "the dullest time on Earth" – or the **Boring Billion**.

DURING
the Boring Billion

BEFORE
the Boring Billion

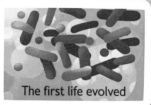

The first life evolved

BORING BILLION

Landmasses moved

Volcanoes erupted

Ice ages hit

There were no significant events

About 1.8 billion years ago

61 A flamingo's perfect nest...

is on a corrosive lake.

Lake Natron, in Tanzania, is one of the most inhospitable environments on Earth. Its waters are deadly, but despite this, 2.5 million flamingos go there every year to breed.

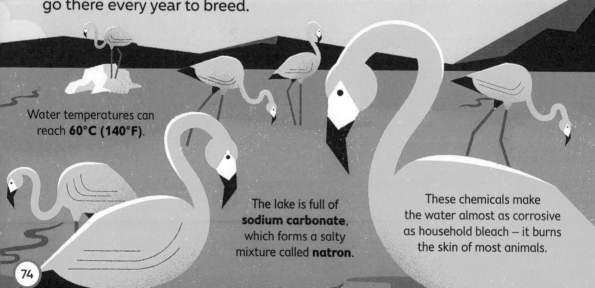

Water temperatures can reach **60°C (140°F)**.

The lake is full of **sodium carbonate**, which forms a salty mixture called **natron**.

These chemicals make the water almost as corrosive as household bleach – it burns the skin of most animals.

BORING
BILLION

BORING
BILLION

AFTER
the Boring Billion

The climate
stayed the same

Nothing really
changed

Complex life evolved

Plants grew on land

Continents were stable

Zzzz

Oceans filled with
creatures

Supercontinents
split up

About 0.8 billion years ago

Islands made of
natron form as the water
evaporates. They're known
as **evaporite islands**.

Flamingos love to eat
tiny organisms called
cyanobacteria, which
thrive in the salty water.
These bacteria turn the lake,
and the flamingos, pink.

Flamingos build their nests on
these islands, where predators,
such as African golden wolves,
can't reach them.

62 Helium is escaping...

and eventually Planet Earth will run out.

The chemical element helium makes up nearly a quarter of the mass of the entire Universe – but there's very little of it to be found on Earth. That's because it's constantly trying to escape into outer space.

Most of Earth's helium is in the form of a gas, created underground when radioactive elements, such as uranium or thorium, decay.

Helium is invisible. It has no smell or taste, and hardly reacts with anything. It is very, very light — and it wants to escape.

Some helium gets caught in reservoirs of natural gas.

Helium gas seeps through cracks in the rock.

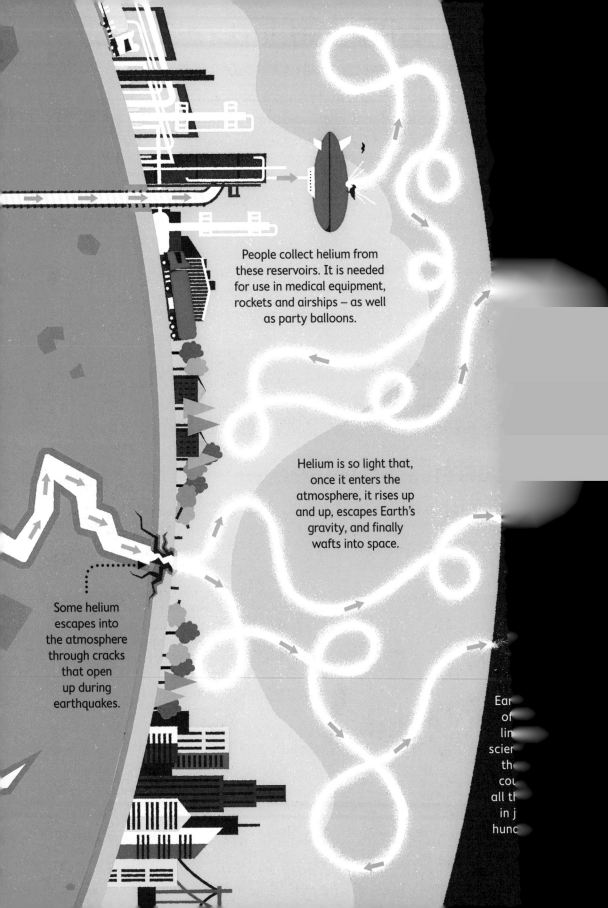

People collect helium from these reservoirs. It is needed for use in medical equipment, rockets and airships – as well as party balloons.

Helium is so light that, once it enters the atmosphere, it rises up and up, escapes Earth's gravity, and finally wafts into space.

Some helium escapes into the atmosphere through cracks that open up during earthquakes.

Ear
of
lin
scie
th
cou
all th
in j
hunc

63 You don't need an umbrella...

to shelter from phantom rain.

When the air on the ground is especially warm, rain drops can evaporate as they fall, so they never reach the ground. Weather experts call this **virga**, but it's also known as **phantom rain**.

Virga can typically be seen in the skies above deserts.

64 Earth is smellier...

after a rainstorm.

Microscopic organisms found in rocks and soil all over the planet constantly release smelly chemicals, called **geosmin**, into the air.

The smell of geosmin is strongest after heavy rain, when the organisms that produce it are carried into the air by tiny water droplets.

The scent of the air after a storm is known as **petrichor**.

Human noses are especially good at picking up this scent, although no one knows exactly why.

65 An underground rainforest...

is growing in the world's largest cave.

Hang Son Doong in Vietnam is the largest cave on Earth. It has a river running through it, and a lush underground rainforest.

The cave was first discovered in 1991, but wasn't explored fully until 2009.

An opening in the ceiling allows sunlight to penetrate the cave.

Here, explorers found a forest, with trees growing up to **30m (100ft)** tall.

Cave height: **200m (660ft)**

The hole in the ceiling provides enough sunlight and rainfall to support an entire rainforest of plants and animals – all under the ground.

Cave width: **150m (490ft)**

66 A vampire and a monster...

came out of a volcano.

On April 10, 1815, a volcano in Southeast Asia produced one of the most powerful eruptions in history. Its after-effects were felt around the world, including dropping temperatures, persistent rainfall, crop failures resulting in food shortages, and even the birth of two new monsters...

A plume of ash and smoke rose up to **43km (27 miles)** high.

That's about four times higher than planes fly.

Darkness spread beneath the cloud for hundreds of miles.

Ash fell from the sky across **Southeast Asia**.

MOUNT TAMBORA

Dutch East Indies (in what is today called Indonesia)

Particles of ash were blown around the world, blocking out sunlight for months.

The global temperature dropped. The next year became known as the **Year Without A Summer**. Harvests failed, leading to a global shortage of food, probably causing hundreds of thousands of deaths.

The boom of the eruption was heard over a thousand miles away, on the island of **Sumatra**.

People as far away as **Paris** and **London** reported unusually bright, vibrant sunsets — caused by particles of ash in the sky.

The bad weather of the Year Without a Summer had an affect on the work artists, writers and musicians produced as well.

A group of writers visiting **Switzerland** wrote scary stories as they sheltered from the rain. **Mary Shelley** came up with *Frankenstein*, a story about a monster created in a science experiment. **John Polidori** wrote *The Vampyre*, the first modern vampire story.

67 North America's highest peak...
has more than 40 names.

Everyone agrees that the highest mountain in North America, standing **6,190m (20,310ft)** above sea level, is a granite peak in Alaska. However, people have long argued about what to call it.

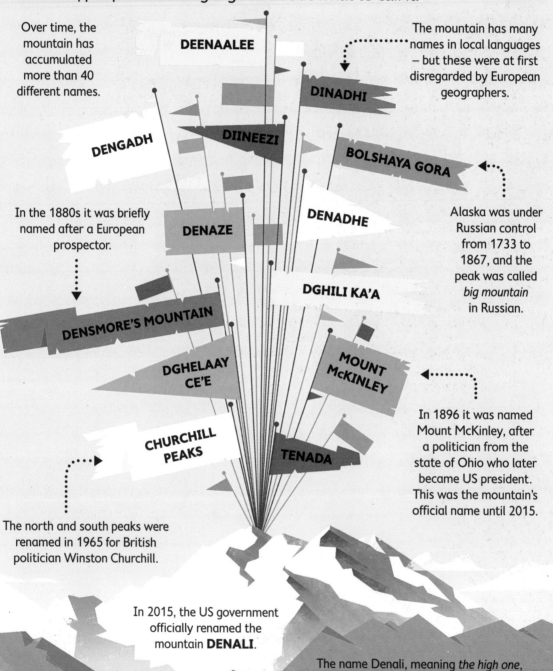

Over time, the mountain has accumulated more than 40 different names.

DEENAALEE

The mountain has many names in local languages – but these were at first disregarded by European geographers.

DINADHI

DIINEEZI

DENGADH

BOLSHAYA GORA

In the 1880s it was briefly named after a European prospector.

DENAZE

DENADHE

Alaska was under Russian control from 1733 to 1867, and the peak was called *big mountain* in Russian.

DGHILI KA'A

DENSMORE'S MOUNTAIN

DGHELAAY CE'E

MOUNT McKINLEY

In 1896 it was named Mount McKinley, after a politician from the state of Ohio who later became US president. This was the mountain's official name until 2015.

CHURCHILL PEAKS

TENADA

The north and south peaks were renamed in 1965 for British politician Winston Churchill.

In 2015, the US government officially renamed the mountain **DENALI**.

The name Denali, meaning *the high one*, has been used by indigenous Alaskan people for thousands of years.

68 Desolation and Despair...

await visitors to the Southern Ocean.

The names given to geographical features, such as mountains and islands, can say more about an explorer's mood than about the place itself.

The waters surrounding Antarctica are scattered with islands. Some are named after explorers – or their friends – or their home towns. Other place names seem to show the emotions of the explorers who discovered them: anxieties, fears, or relief.

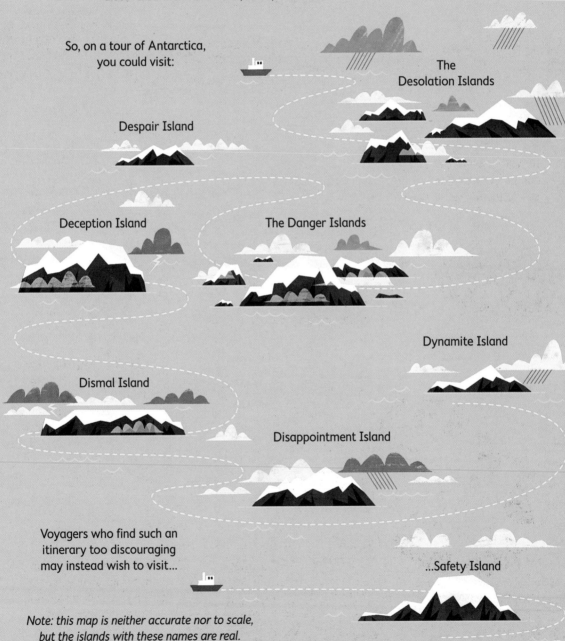

So, on a tour of Antarctica, you could visit:

The Desolation Islands

Despair Island

Deception Island

The Danger Islands

Dynamite Island

Dismal Island

Disappointment Island

Voyagers who find such an itinerary too discouraging may instead wish to visit...

...Safety Island

Note: this map is neither accurate nor to scale, but the islands with these names are real.

69 Sailing stones...

drift across the desert at night.

In Death Valley, California, there's an area called the Racetrack Playa where large, heavy stones seem to move by themselves, overnight. The stones, which are far too heavy to lift, are known as sailing stones.

So how do they move? Scientists began researching the stones in the early 1900s, but it wasn't until 2014 that the mystery was finally solved...

At night temperatures drop, and a thin layer of ice forms across the Racetrack Playa.

As the ice begins to melt in the early morning sun, it floats on a shallow layer of water.

Even the gentlest breeze is enough to move the floating ice, carrying the stones with it.

The scorching desert sun then dries up any water, leaving the sailing stones in their new positions.

70 Crystals as big as buses...

are growing inside a Mexican cave.

Beneath the cave lies hot, molten rock called magma, which makes the cave so hot it can only be explored for a few minutes at a time.

Phew, it's over **50°C (122°F)** in here.

The heat has slowly evaporated sulfurous water in the cave, leaving behind crystals of a substance called **selenite**.

Over 500,000 years, the crystals have grown into colossal structures.

4m (13ft)

The crystals are among the largest ever found on Earth. Some of them grow to the size of a small bus.

12m (39ft)

Woah...

Right now, the cave is flooded and inaccessible. This means new crystals will be forming.

71 Hollywood snow...

once came from the Californian desert.

In the golden age of Hollywood movie-making, in the 1930s and 1940s, winter scenes were filmed all year round using fake snow – made of a mineral called **gypsum**.

Gypsum was mined in the desert...

driven to Los Angeles...

shaved into snowy white flakes...

Other classic movie substitutes for snow included salt, sugar, soap flakes, marble dust, and cornflakes painted white.

...and sprinkled onto movie sets.

72 Many, many mini moons...

orbit Earth at any time.

Earth has only one Moon – but thousands of tiny, fast-moving asteroids also orbit our planet as mini moons. Most are much smaller than a family car and, so far, none has stayed in place for very long.

Asteroids can become entangled in Earth's gravity and, for a while, fall into orbit around the planet.

Such mini moons are known as **temporarily captured orbiters**, or TCOs.

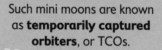

Hey! I'm the only REAL moon around here!

On average, TCOs spend about **nine months** in orbit around Earth.

Eventually they spiral into the atmosphere and burn up, or land unnoticed, or spin away into space.

animals get smaller.

ANIMALS SHRINKING!

Scientists have noticed an unexpected consequence of climate change. Average temperatures are rising, and as they do the average sizes of many kinds of animals, over time, are getting smaller. Our nature correspondent tells us more...

Lots of types of fish, including tuna, salmon and cod, are becoming smaller. Some scientists think they'll shrink by 30% for every 1°C the water heats up.

Pah, they don't make 'em like they used to.

Chamois goats are about 25% smaller than they were just 30 years ago.

12°C (54°F)

13°C (55.5°F)

14°C (57°F)

Not for the first time!

55 million years ago, Earth heated up quickly. Fossils show that during this period, called the Paleocene-Eocene Thermal Maximum, the size of ancient mammals shrank by around a third.

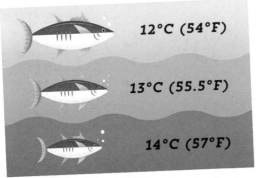

WHY IS THIS HAPPENING?

Warm water has less oxygen in it than cold water, so large fish won't have enough oxygen to breathe. As small fish need less oxygen, they will survive.

Larger animals find it harder to cool down, so in a hot climate it is better to be smaller.

Small animals need less food. As the climate heats up and some animals die out, those that need less food have a better chance of survival.

WEATHER FORECAST			
The hot weather is set to continue.	MON	TUES	WED

All the gold mined on Earth...

came from outer space.

Gold is a **heavy metal** – a metal that is dense and weighs a lot for its size. It can't be formed on Earth, but is created inside stars as they burn. So scientists think the gold mined on Earth must have come from space.

There is some gold in Earth's *core*. Scientists think there was some gold in the cosmic dust that clumped together when Earth first formed, but it sank into the molten middle of the planet, where it is out of reach.

Scientists think the gold in Earth's *crust* came from gold-encrusted meteorites, which crashed here in a period called the Late Heavy Bombardment, about 4 billion years ago.

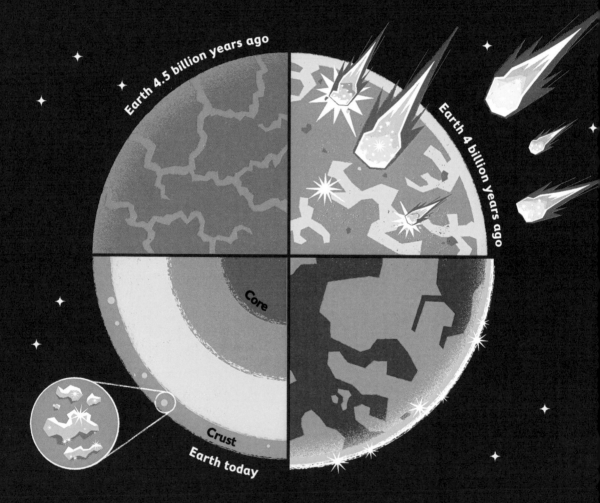

Earth 4.5 billion years ago

Earth 4 billion years ago

Core

Crust

Earth today

Only a billionth of Earth's crust is gold. That doesn't sound like much, but it's been enough to mine all the gold ever used.

The gold in Earth's core is much more plentiful. Scientists think there's enough there to coat the planet in a gold layer nearly 4m (13ft) thick, but it's impossible to get at.

75 Pterosaurs couldn't fly...

in 21st century skies.

The largest flying animals alive today are birds called albatrosses. They can stay up in the air because the gases making up Earth's atmosphere are just thick and hot enough for their enormous wings to push against.

Wandering albatross
Wingspan: up to 4m (13ft)
Weight: up to 12.7kg (28lb)

Millions of years ago, during the Jurassic and Cretaceous periods, the skies were filled with flying reptiles called pterosaurs – creatures *much larger* than an albatross.

Quetzalcoatlus (the largest ever pterosaur)
Wingspan: up to 14m (46ft)
Weight: up to 250kg (550lb)

Experts think that, in order for these massive creatures to stay aloft, the atmosphere must have been much thicker and warmer than it is now.
BUT...

Wait – what's wrong with me?!

...in today's thinner, cooler atmosphere, a pterosaur would *never* get off the ground – no matter how hard it flapped its wings.

What's the matter old timer? Having some trouble taking off?

76 A future president...

turned the American west into a chessboard.

The US began in 1776 as just thirteen states on the eastern coast of North America. The nation expanded rapidly, gaining vast regions in the west. The US government urgently needed a way to map and organize these lands, so that they could be sold to settlers and investors.

Thomas Jefferson, a politician from Virginia who later became US President, had a solution: to divide the land into an orderly grid.

Jefferson's scheme – known as the **Public Land Survey System** (PLSS) – was put in place in 1785. Surveyors catalogued *millions* of square miles.

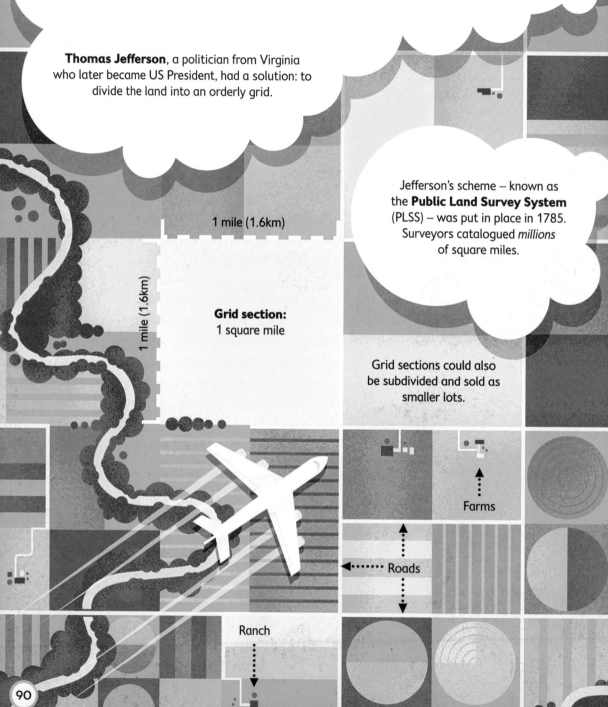

1 mile (1.6km)

1 mile (1.6km)

Grid section:
1 square mile

Grid sections could also be subdivided and sold as smaller lots.

Farms

Roads

Ranch

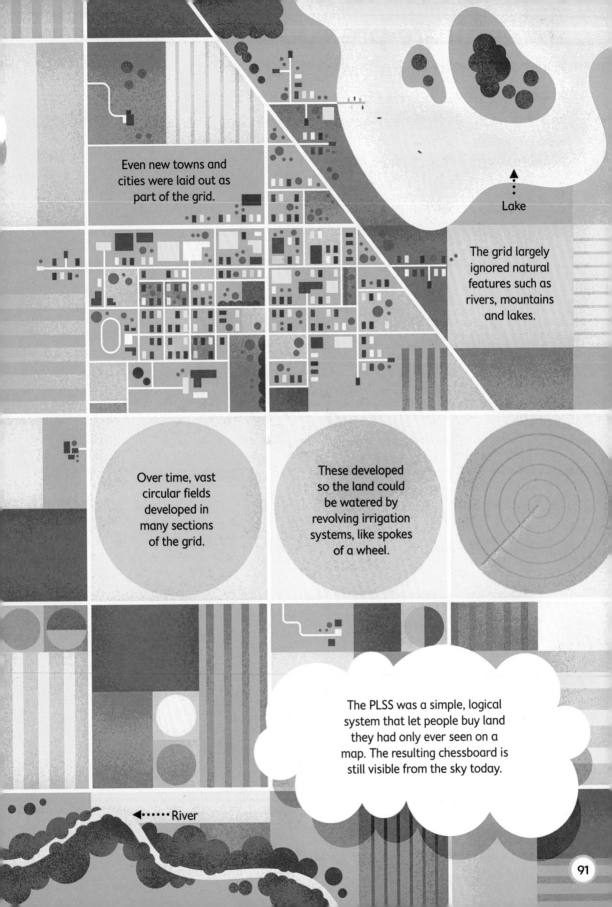

Even new towns and cities were laid out as part of the grid.

Lake

The grid largely ignored natural features such as rivers, mountains and lakes.

Over time, vast circular fields developed in many sections of the grid.

These developed so the land could be watered by revolving irrigation systems, like spokes of a wheel.

The PLSS was a simple, logical system that let people buy land they had only ever seen on a map. The resulting chessboard is still visible from the sky today.

River

77 A third man...

haunts climbers on the highest peaks.

Humans can't survive for long in the cold air of the world's highest mountain peaks. At extreme altitudes, climbers suffer from a range of deadly illnesses – and a mysterious hallucination known as **third man syndrome**.

Climbers pushing past **8,000m (26,000ft)** enter what's known as the **Death Zone**, where the body absorbs just one third of the oxygen available at sea level.

Death
Zone

8,000m
26,000ft

Oxygen starvation causes headaches, fatigue, nausea, sleeplessness, confusion, and potentially fatal swelling of the brain or lungs.

Many climbers at high altitude also report seeing or feeling a mysterious figure accompanying them on the slopes.

But the mysterious companion whispering good – or bad – advice isn't real. It's a hallucination: their own brains leading them astray.

This **third man syndrome** fades when climbers return to lower altitudes.

78 Costumes, wigs and props...

were once essential on polar expeditions.

In the 19th century, polar explorers sailed into the Arctic Circle in search of new sea routes, uncharted islands and the North Pole. They took with them everything necessary for survival – including stage props and costumes.

What made these items so essential is that, near the Earth's poles, the Sun sinks below the horizon for six months of the year.

Explorers found that the sea would freeze as the cold, dark winter months approached – halting their progress. The water would often stay frozen from August until June.

As a result, expedition ships could spend ten months of the year locked in ice, unable to sail, until the sea would briefly thaw again.

| Jan | Feb | Mar | Apr | May | Jun | Jul | Aug | Sep | Oct | Nov | Dec |

Spending months shut up in cold, cramped vessels, men could become bored, morose and cranky – and their mental health would have suffered.

So, to keep up morale, explorers put on plays, gave lectures and played concerts for their crewmates.

79 A fleet of rubber ducks...

helped to track how the oceans move.

In 1992, a shipping container transporting 29,000 yellow ducks and other bath toys was broken in a storm, plunging its contents into the Pacific Ocean. Oceanographers have since used these toys as trackers, following their journeys to find out more about ocean currents.

1 Ocean currents carried about 19,000 toys south. These eventually washed up in Australia, Indonesia and South America. The rest drifted north...

2 1993 – 400 toys reached the coast of Alaska, **3,200km (2,000 miles)** from the spill site.

3 1995 – more toys were found frozen in Arctic ice, **4,500km (2,800 miles)** from the spill site.

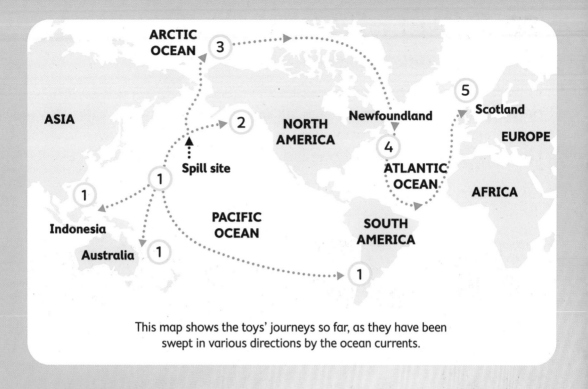

This map shows the toys' journeys so far, as they have been swept in various directions by the ocean currents.

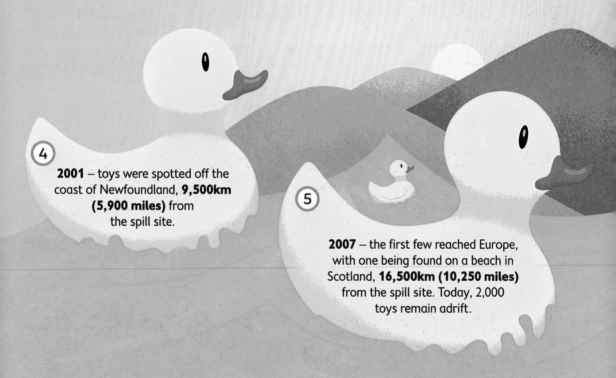

4 **2001** – toys were spotted off the coast of Newfoundland, **9,500km (5,900 miles)** from the spill site.

5 **2007** – the first few reached Europe, with one being found on a beach in Scotland, **16,500km (10,250 miles)** from the spill site. Today, 2,000 toys remain adrift.

Oceanographers usually use floating electronic trackers, sending out about one thousand trackers at a time. Because there were so many floating toys, they have helped scientists build up a much more detailed picture of the movement of the planet's seas and oceans.

80 The Black Death...

made the planet colder.

Between the 17th and 19th centuries, temperatures around the world dropped significantly. Historians call this the **Little Ice Age**. Scientists think the climate was, in part, affected by a drop in the global population, after a devastating plague called the **Black Death**.

Tens of millions of people died in the Black Death, a plague that spread across west Asia and Europe in the 14th century.

The plague wiped out over 20% of the world's population. It left lots of towns and villages empty.

Abandoned villages went to ruin, and during the next couple of centuries trees took over, in a process known as **reforestation**.

All those extra trees took up lots of carbon dioxide, which in turn cooled the climate. Modern studies of soil support this theory.

This is just one part of the story. It's likely that changes in ocean circulation and lower levels of radiation from the Sun also contributed towards the Little Ice Age.

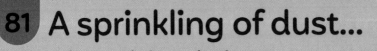

81 A sprinkling of dust...

can melt an Alpine glacier.

Clean, white snow reflects back about 90% of the sunlight that strikes it, so glaciers can stay cool and frozen year after year. But just a thin layer of dust can darken a glacier's surface – and seal its fate.

1 Tiny particles of soot and dust can float high up into the atmosphere.

2 Some of these particles settle on glaciers – large masses of ice that flow very slowly downhill.

3 The darker, dusty surfaces reflect less light, so they absorb more heat, which makes them start to melt slowly.

4 The glaciers in the European Alps began to melt in the 1850s — when steam trains and factories began spewing soot into the air.

These glaciers are still melting and shrinking today.

make deadly volcanoes even more dangerous.

Volcanic eruptions can produce massive explosions, fountains of lava, and thundering cascades of hot gas, rock and ash. But they can be dangerous in other ways, too.

Look out! That volcano is erupting! Can you choose a path to safety?

A B C D E

Creeping vog surrounds you!

Sulfurous volcanic gases seep out into the air and mix with water droplets, forming vog: an acidic, throat-burning, skin-irritating, eye-watering volcanic smog.

You stumble into the billowing laze!

A river of lava pours into the sea and boils up into billowing clouds. This deadly lava haze, or laze, is filled with **hydrochloric acid** and razor-sharp particles of glass.

Pele tangles you in her hair and cuts you from within!

Lava bubbles burst, releasing strands of glass so fine and light they float on the wind. Called **Pele's hair**, after the Hawaiian goddess of fire, the golden strands shimmer, shine – and shatter easily...

Beware of breathing or drinking these miniscule shards!

A whirling lavanado reduces you to cinders!

The intense heat of the lava flow creates gusting, swirling updrafts. These are so strong that they pull fiery tornadoes of spattering lava (lavanadoes) up into the air.

Congratulations!

You're slightly scorched, lightly poached, mildly toasted, but you survived!

99

are separated by a few miles of icy seawater.

Out in the cold, windswept sea between Alaska and Russia lie two barren rocks known as Yesterday Island and Tomorrow Island. They are located just **3.8km (2.4 miles)** apart – but are separated by **21 hours**.

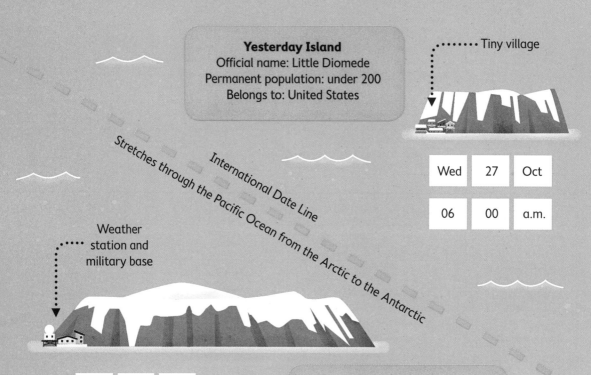

Yesterday Island
Official name: Little Diomede
Permanent population: under 200
Belongs to: United States

Tiny village

Wed	27	Oct
06	00	a.m.

International Date Line
Stretches through the Pacific Ocean from the Arctic to the Antarctic

Weather station and military base

Thurs	28	Oct
03	00	a.m.

Tomorrow Island
Official name: Big Diomede
Permanent population: 0
Belongs to: Russia

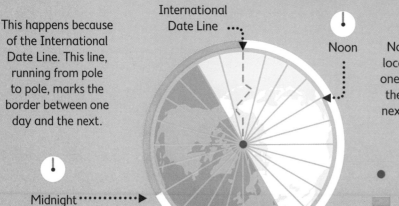

This happens because of the International Date Line. This line, running from pole to pole, marks the border between one day and the next.

International Date Line

Noon

No matter what the local time may be, it's one day on one side of the date line and the next day on the other.

Midnight

- NORTH POLE
- WEDNESDAY
- THURSDAY

84 Friday, Saturday and Sunday...

can happen all at once.

1 The International Date Line isn't a straight line from pole to pole. To avoid splitting countries in half, the line actually zigzags across the globe, around country boundaries.

Kiritimati (Christmas Island)

International Date Line in South Pacific

2 So it veers thousands of miles off course (as shown here) to loop around the Pacific islands that make up the nation of Kiribati.

3 As a result, for about two hours every day, it is simultaneously three dates at once — today, yesterday, and tomorrow — at different locations around the world.

American Samoa

4 For example, all at the same time, it will be:
11:30 p.m. in American Samoa on January 1
10:30 a.m. in London on January 2
12:30 a.m. on Christmas Island on January 3

Hey, what time is it?

Um, that depends... Where are we?

In the winter, the sea between Big Diomede and Little Diomede sometimes freezes solid.

So you *could* walk from Tomorrow to Yesterday... and back again.

A prehistoric network of caves...

was carved out by giant sloths.

Caves normally form when water wears down rock, but scientists have found over 1,500 caves and networks of tunnels in South America that seem to have been created differently.

Scientists have noticed that the tunnels are covered in strange scratch marks...

...and have wavy, domed ceilings, which couldn't have been formed by water.

These unusual features suggest that the tunnels, known as **paleoburrows**, were dug as shelters over 10,000 years ago by massive prehistoric creatures, probably giant sloths.

The unique shape of the caves is a result of sloths digging...

...then resting...

...before clawing out a new section of tunnel.

Giant sloths, **now extinct**, were about the same size and weight as an elephant.

Fossilized chicken bones...

will leave a lasting record of human existence.

Distinct layers of rock build up over time. Scientists studying what makes up each layer can see the differences that mark one epoch (see page 38) from the next. Some experts think humans are creating a new epoch, known as the **Anthropocene.**

The food people eat is likely to leave some of the most widespread evidence of human activity on Earth.

Industrial-scale farming methods have produced chickens that are much **larger** than their ancestors.

All around the world, people throw away the bones of **60 billion** of these chickens each year.

Thousands of years from now, scientists will find layers of rock containing the remains of lots of large fossilized chicken bones.

The remains of these bones, as well as **technofossils** made of waste materials, such as plastic and concrete, will provide rocky evidence of the Anthropocene.

Older layers of rock will reveal far smaller and far fewer chicken bones, and won't contain technofossils...

...marking a time before human activity dominated Earth.

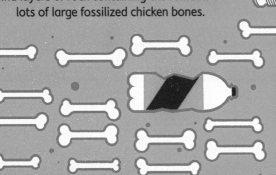

Even deeper layers will reveal dinosaur fossils from epochs long before humans or chickens roamed the planet.

87 The greatest threat to life...

is humans.

Five times in the history of the planet, a large number of the species on Earth have died out quickly, in what scientists call **mass extinctions**. These were caused by sudden changes in climate or atmosphere. Scientists now think we're in the middle of a sixth, and this time the cause is humans.

This map shows some of the ways that human activity is causing extinctions.

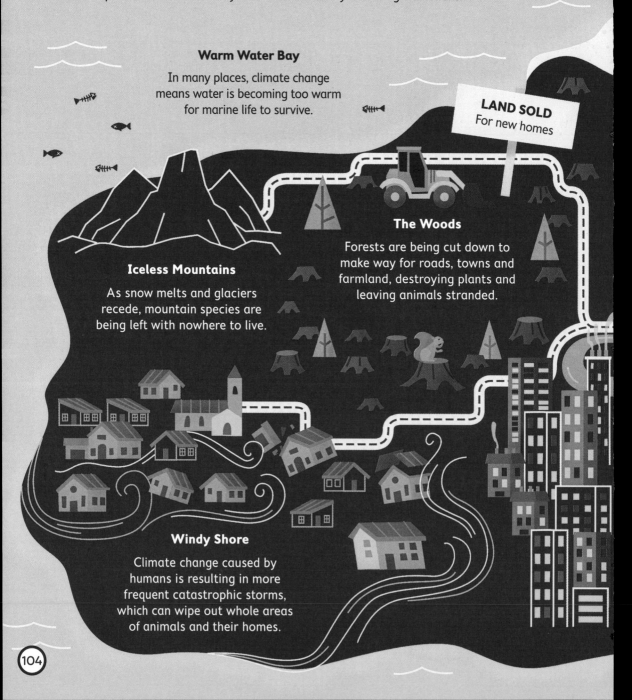

Warm Water Bay

In many places, climate change means water is becoming too warm for marine life to survive.

LAND SOLD
For new homes

The Woods

Forests are being cut down to make way for roads, towns and farmland, destroying plants and leaving animals stranded.

Iceless Mountains

As snow melts and glaciers recede, mountain species are being left with nowhere to live.

Windy Shore

Climate change caused by humans is resulting in more frequent catastrophic storms, which can wipe out whole areas of animals and their homes.

Dead Reef

Coral reefs are dying as seas warm up.

Routes blocked

Roads criss-crossing the countryside block important routes for animals, so animals end up separated from each other, food and water.

STOP
Path blocked ahead

Dusty Desert

More and more of the world is turning to desert, as temperatures increase and less rain falls in hot places.

Big City

Towns and cities are spreading into surrounding countryside every day, destroying habitats.

Toxic River

Waste running out of cities is making many bodies of water too polluted for fish to live in.

It's hard to put exact figures on this extinction event. But most scientists agree that the extinction rate is

100 to **1,000 times**

higher than it would be without human actions, so it's important that people work to stop the damage that's being caused.

There could be a new continent...

submerged beneath the sea.

There are seven continents on Earth. But an eighth, called **Zealandia**, might be added to the list. It's not currently recognized as a continent, but some geologists think it fulfils all the criteria required to qualify...

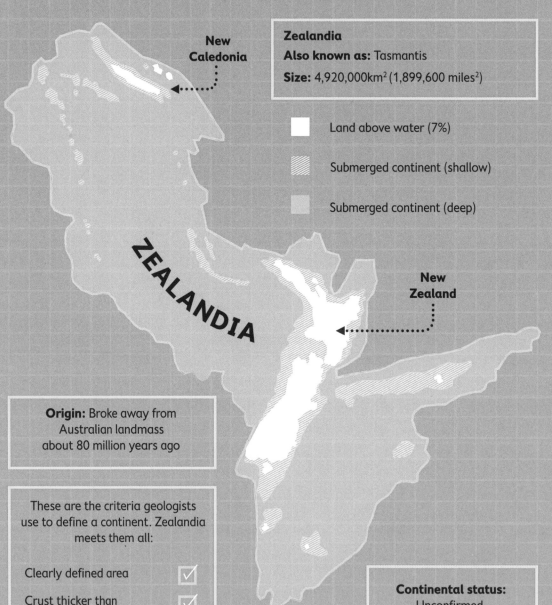

New Caledonia

Zealandia
Also known as: Tasmantis
Size: 4,920,000km² (1,899,600 miles²)

☐ Land above water (7%)

▨ Submerged continent (shallow)

☐ Submerged continent (deep)

ZEALANDIA

New Zealand

Origin: Broke away from Australian landmass about 80 million years ago

These are the criteria geologists use to define a continent. Zealandia meets them all:

Clearly defined area ☑

Crust thicker than the ocean floor ☑

Distinctive geology ☑

Area more than 1 million km² (386,100 miles²) ☑

Continental status: Unconfirmed. Most authorities, including the United Nations, claim that continents must actually consist of dry land.

89 Bright blue fire...

spews from an Indonesian volcano.

The Kawah Ijen volcano complex in East Java, Indonesia, is unique.

Instead of the fiery reds and oranges seen in other volcanoes, Ijen's eruptions are electric blue.

The rock in the region is high in a chemical called **sulfur**. The high temperature of the volcano turns this into a gas.

When the gas reaches the surface, it mixes with oxygen in the air and catches fire – burning with a bright blue flame.

Some of the sulfur cools to become a liquid. It flows down the sides of the volcano, still burning – so it looks like blue lava.

90 One of Tutankhamun's gems...

was created by a meteorite strike.

When archaeologists discovered the tomb of the Egyptian king Tutankhamun in 1922, they found a pendant. It is filled with precious jewels – including one in the middle made from Libyan desert glass, formed by a meteorite impact 20 million years ago.

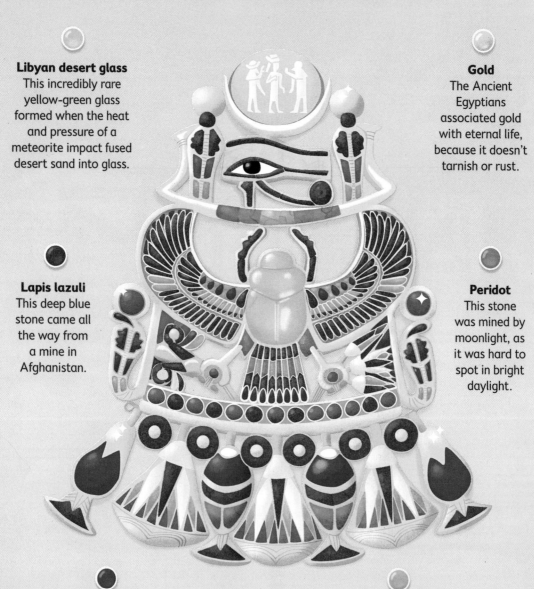

Libyan desert glass
This incredibly rare yellow-green glass formed when the heat and pressure of a meteorite impact fused desert sand into glass.

Gold
The Ancient Egyptians associated gold with eternal life, because it doesn't tarnish or rust.

Lapis lazuli
This deep blue stone came all the way from a mine in Afghanistan.

Peridot
This stone was mined by moonlight, as it was hard to spot in bright daylight.

Carnelian
The Ancient Egyptians prized this red-orange gemstone, which they associated with the Sun.

Turquoise
By the turquoise mines at Serabit el-Khadim the Ancient Egyptians built a temple to Hathor, a goddess known as the turquoise lady.

91 Ultramarine blue...

was once more valuable than gold.

Lapis lazuli, a precious gemstone, was once prized by artists. They ground it down to make a uniquely brilliant blue pigment, known as ultramarine, that was used to make paint. For centuries, ultramarine was the most costly paint in the world.

Up until the 18th century the Sar-i Sang mine, in what is now Afghanistan, was the *only known* place that produced lapis lazuli.

Turning lapis lazuli into ultramarine was a long and difficult process, and only very small quantities of the pigment were produced.

Because it was so rare, and because its blue shade was so pure, many artists used ultramarine only for important subjects, especially in religious paintings.

Michelangelo, a 16th-century Italian artist, left his painting *The Entombment* unfinished, because he was unable to afford enough ultramarine – and refused to use an inferior blue in its place.

92 Chimborazo beats Everest...

to be the highest point on Earth.

Mount Everest is generally considered the tallest mountain on the planet, as it's the highest point above sea level. But if you measure from the middle of Earth's core, the highest point is actually Mount Chimborazo. That's because Earth isn't actually a sphere. It's an **oblate spheroid** – which means it bulges around the Equator.

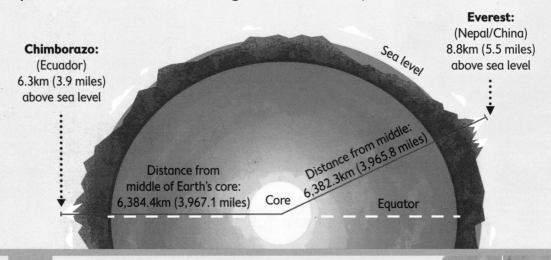

Everest:
(Nepal/China)
8.8km (5.5 miles)
above sea level

Sea level

Chimborazo:
(Ecuador)
6.3km (3.9 miles)
above sea level

Distance from middle of Earth's core:
6,384.4km (3,967.1 miles)

Distance from middle:
6,382.3km (3,965.8 miles)

Core

Equator

93 Living bridges grow...

in the wettest place on Earth.

Record amounts of rain fall in the north east of India each year. Wooden structures rot quickly in the downpours, so the locals build bridges out of living trees instead.

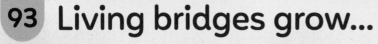

First, they build a bamboo frame.

Then, they tie roots of living fig trees to the frame.

Over time, the tough, flexible roots grow across the river, forming a living bridge.

These bridges can take over ten years to grow, but last for centuries.

94 Two of Earth's largest rivers...

don't mix when they meet.

In Manaus, Brazil, the blackish water of the Rio Negro meets the pale water of the Amazon River, but the two do not mix immediately. Differences in temperature, density and speed form an invisible barrier between the rivers.

Amazon River

Rio Negro

Mud and silt from the Andes Mountains make this water dense and sandy.

Decayed plants dissolve into this water, making it dark but very clear.

Up to 6km (3.7 miles) per hour

22°C (72°F)

2km (1.2 miles) per hour

28°C (82°F)

The rivers remain separated for **6km (3.7 miles)**

Eventually, islands in the water cause swirling currents, called eddies...

...which force the two rivers to churn together.

The mixed water then flows as the Amazon River for 1,500km (930 miles) to the Atlantic Ocean.

95 Super corals...

could save the world's reefs.

Climate change is heating the oceans, causing coral reefs around the world to die, in a process known as **bleaching**. One way scientists are trying to save the reefs is by breeding stronger corals that are more resistant to warm waters, which they call **super corals**.

Scientists go to areas where corals are bleaching and dying.

They extract corals that have survived and breed them again and again, creating super-strong new corals.

Scientists think they could also treat these corals with a type of bacteria that would help them survive oil spills.

The new, improved super corals are then planted back into the sea, and form the start of a new reef.

Coral reefs make up just 0.2% of the ocean, but provide homes for 25% of its life. Without radical and widespread conservation, reefs might die out completely in the next 30 years.

96 Rogue waves...

are common but unpredictable and unexplained.

Sailors have long told of freakishly large waves that strike without warning on the open sea, sinking ships in a matter of seconds. No one really believed them – until New Year's Day of 1995.

New Year's Day 1995: Instruments on the Draupner oil platform, off the coast of Norway, measured the impact of a weirdly massive wave – by far the biggest ever recorded.

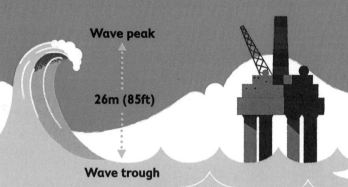

Wave peak

26m (85ft)

Wave trough

This, at last, was evidence that rogue waves – waves more than twice as large as those around them – really do exist.

Scientists have since confirmed that such waves are relatively common.

Oceanographers don't know exactly how rogue waves become so big. It may have to do with subtle shifts in **winds** and **currents**, and with large waves overlapping and joining forces.

Winds

Currents

Rogue waves are thought to have destroyed untold numbers of vessels over the years – and even low-flying aircraft such as rescue helicopters.

97 An iron curtain...

created a green belt.

From 1945 to around 1990, a barrier known as the **Iron Curtain** ran for hundreds of miles through Europe, dividing East from West. It was defended with guard towers, barbed wire and minefields – but alongside them, nature flourished.

The barrier was built during the **Cold War**, a period when rival governments in Eastern and Western Europe teetered on the edge of a world war.

Guard tower

Whinchats

Landmines

It created a long, narrow strip of land free from farming, construction and most human activity – providing a haven for some 600 species of rare plants and animals.

Barbed wire

Moor frogs

Pearl mussels

Black storks

The Iron Curtain was meant to stop spies, saboteurs and refugees from crossing the border between the two sides.

Red-backed shrikes

Tank

Otters

Machine gun bunker

Ladyslipper orchids

Today, the Iron Curtain has gone, and people can cross freely where it used to be – but much of the land remains a nature reserve: a long, lush, green strip of wilderness.

98 Desert dust fertilizes...
the Amazon Rainforest.

In the Sahara Desert in Africa, there's a place called the Bodélé Depression that used to be a lake.

Microscopic organisms from the lake are buried in the dust there, filling it with nourishing chemicals.

Every year, a vast amount of dust is blown from the Bodélé Depression out west over the Atlantic Ocean.

A lot of it falls into the water, but some is blown **5,000km (3,100 miles)** across the ocean.

The dust that arrives in South America falls onto the Amazon Rainforest. It is full of a chemical called phosphorus, that fertilizes plants and helps them grow.

This almost exactly replaces the amount of phosphorus that is washed out of the soil by heavy tropical rains. Without these deposits from the Sahara, the rainforest wouldn't be able to grow.

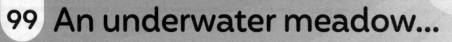

99 An underwater meadow...

is older than the pyramids.

One of the oldest living things on Earth is a seagrass meadow growing in the Mediterranean Sea. It is a type of seagrass called *Posidonia oceanica*, which lives a very long time. In fact, this meadow is older than most of human history.

When scientists tested a seagrass meadow over a span of **15km (9.3 miles)**, they found that even though it looked like thousands of individual plants, the entire meadow was, in fact, a single living organism.

Based on its size and the speed at which seagrass grows, scientists estimated that the meadow they tested was up to **200,000 years old**. This makes the meadow older than...

The Eiffel Tower
— completed in **1889**

The Parthenon of Athens
— around **2,500** years old

Posidonia oceanica reproduces by making exact copies of itself — a process known as **cloning**.

The identical clones making up the seagrass meadow count as a single organism because they all share a single root system.

The Pyramids — around **4,500** years old

The extinction of woolly mammoths — around **15,000** years ago, when the meadow was already **185,000 years old!**

Life on Earth won't last forever...

but *how* it ends is a matter of chance.

In several billion years, the Sun is likely to grow into a type of star known as a red giant, burning away Earth's atmosphere and boiling off the oceans. But things could go badly wrong before then, too...

You could use dice to play your way through the **RINGS OF DOOM!**

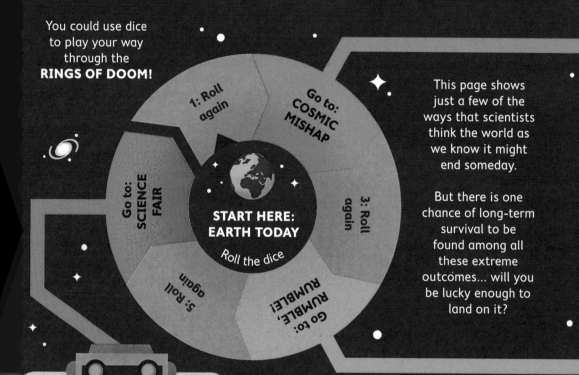

START HERE: EARTH TODAY

Roll the dice

1: Roll again

Go to: COSMIC MISHAP

3: Roll again

Go to: RUMBLE, RUMBLE!

5: Roll again

Go to: SCIENCE FAIR

This page shows just a few of the ways that scientists think the world as we know it might end someday.

But there is one chance of long-term survival to be found among all these extreme outcomes... will you be lucky enough to land on it?

ROBOT OVERLORDS
Artificial intelligence becomes more and more advanced. Computers become self-aware and enslave humans.

SPACE ELEVATOR
Scientists build a space elevator to lift heavy spacecraft into orbit. Then we LEAVE EARTH to explore and settle the Universe.

SCIENCE FAIR
Let's invent some new technologies!

Go to: ROBOT OVERLORDS

3: Roll again

1: Roll again

Go to: NANOBOTS

Go to: SPACE ELEVATOR

5: Roll again

GAMMA RAY BURST

Two nearby stars collide, generating a beam of devastating gamma rays.

This strips away Earth's protective ozone layer and bombards us with radiation.

ALIEN INVASION

Scientists think it's likely that millions of alien civilizations exist in our galaxy. If one ever makes contact, it may not come in peace...

COSMIC MISHAP
It came from outer space!

Go to: GAMMA RAY BURST

3: Roll again

1: Roll again

Go to: ALIEN INVASION

Go to: ROGUE PLANET HITS

5: Roll again

ROGUE PLANET HITS

A vast, wayward planet hurtles into the Solar System, heading straight for Earth. Kaboom!

SUPERVOLCANO

A massive eruption spews ash into the atmosphere, plunging the Earth into darkness for years.

WAIT

Isn't there something *much more urgent* we should be worrying about?
Go to: PAGES 104–105

BIG RED BUTTON

Nuclear war breaks out. Cities and forests burn. Nuclear fallout blankets the Earth.

ROGUE PLANET MISSES

A vast, wayward planet hurtles past, and its gravity pulls Earth out of orbit. We go spinning into the interstellar void.

Go to: SUPER-VOLCANO

1: Roll again

3: Roll again

RUMBLE, RUMBLE
Wait, why is the ground shaking?

NANOBOTS

Self-replicating nanobots (microscopic robots that make copies of themselves) go haywire, multiplying endlessly and covering Earth in a lifeless goo.

Go to: ROGUE PLANET MISSES

5: Roll again

Go to: BIG RED BUTTON

Where on Earth?

The numbers on this map of the world show the locations of some of the "100 things" described in this book.

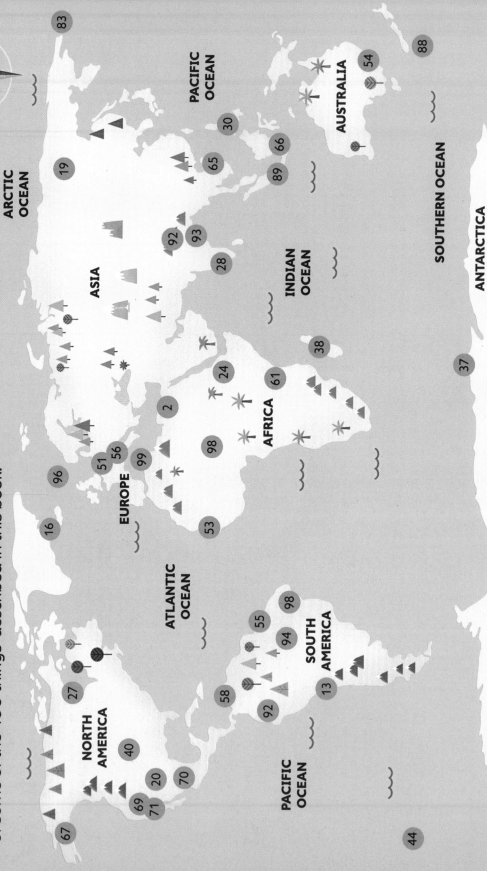

10 things to do...
to protect Planet Earth.

Human activity is causing enormous harm to our planet, but there are lots of things people can do to reduce that harm. Here are just a few...

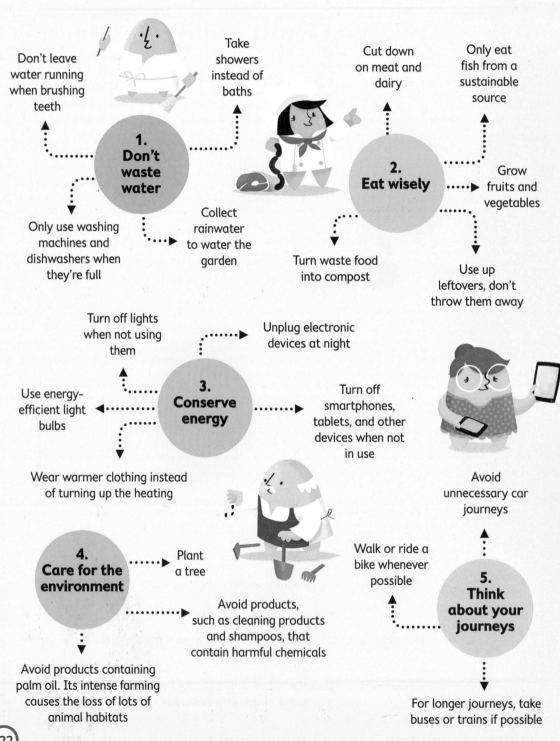

Don't leave water running when brushing teeth

Take showers instead of baths

Cut down on meat and dairy

Only eat fish from a sustainable source

1. Don't waste water

2. Eat wisely

Grow fruits and vegetables

Only use washing machines and dishwashers when they're full

Collect rainwater to water the garden

Turn waste food into compost

Use up leftovers, don't throw them away

Turn off lights when not using them

Unplug electronic devices at night

3. Conserve energy

Use energy-efficient light bulbs

Turn off smartphones, tablets, and other devices when not in use

Wear warmer clothing instead of turning up the heating

Avoid unnecessary car journeys

4. Care for the environment

Plant a tree

Walk or ride a bike whenever possible

5. Think about your journeys

Avoid products, such as cleaning products and shampoos, that contain harmful chemicals

Avoid products containing palm oil. Its intense farming causes the loss of lots of animal habitats

For longer journeys, take buses or trains if possible

Reuse plastic bags

Use a reusable water bottle

Old electronic devices can be used to make new ones

6. Reuse

7. Recycle

Use rechargable batteries

Give old, unwanted devices or toys to friends or to charity

Recycle glass and cans – it often takes less energy to recycle lots of cans than to make one new one

Wrap gifts in old newspaper or magazines

Use cloth or paper shopping bags instead of plastic ones

Talk to friends, family, and teachers about being environmentally friendly

8. Talk, inform, volunteer

9. Reduce

Choose products with less packaging – especially plastic

Find local environmental groups, take part in community clean-up projects

Avoid using plastic drinking straws

Avoid using plastic knives, forks and spoons

10. Find out more

For more ideas on ways to help protect the planet, visit the Usborne Quicklinks website for links to sites with videos, facts and activities.

Here are some of the things you can do at the sites we recommend:

• Discover ways to help Planet Earth – starting now!

• Quiz your knowledge about ocean pollution, endangered animals and more

• See how kids are raising awareness and taking care of the environment

• Explore ways to help wildlife

• Find out more about our changing planet with video clips and helpful facts

Go to usborne.com/Quicklinks and enter the keywords:
things to know about planet earth

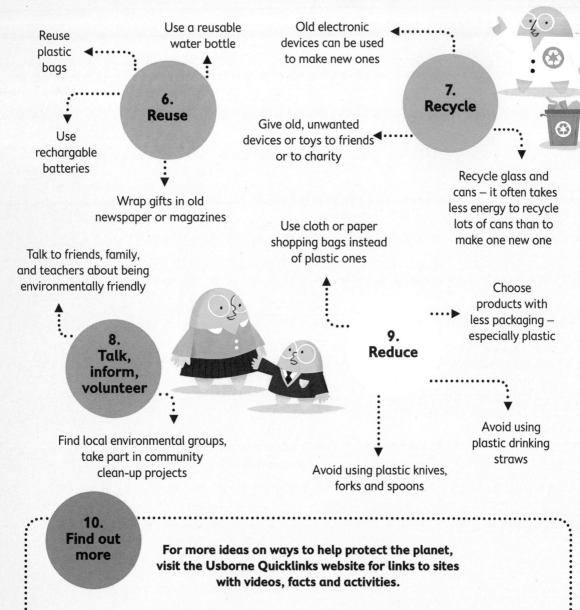

Glossary

This glossary explains some of the words used in this book.
Words written in *italic* type have their own entries.

altitude Height above sea level

Antarctic The icy region of Earth around the South Pole

Arctic The icy region of Earth around the North Pole

asteroid A small rock that orbits a star

atmosphere A mixture of gases that surrounds Earth and some other planets

axis An imaginary line between the North and South *poles*, around which Earth spins

barren Infertile; not producing vegetation

cartographer A map maker

cell The basic unit of living things

climate The typical or average weather conditions in a particular region

climate change The change in Earth's *climate* over time

conservationists Scientists and campaigners working to protect and preserve *species* and their *environments*

continent A major land mass

coral reef A structure made up of the skeletons of small sea animals called coral polyps

core The central part of a body such as a planet

crater A hollow area created by a volcanic *eruption* or the impact of a lump of rock such as a *meteorite*

crust Earth's solid outer layer

current The movement of water or air in a definite direction, often through a stiller surrounding body

desert A region that is very dry, with under 250mm (9.8in) of rainfall per year

earthquake The sudden fracturing of rock which sends waves of energy through the ground, making it shake

endangered species A *species* that is at serious risk of *extinction*

endemic Native to a particular place

environment The surrounding conditions in which living things exist

Equator An imaginary line around the middle of the Earth, dividing north and south

eruption The ejection of *lava*, rocks, hot ash and gases from a *volcano*

extinction When the last member of a *species* dies, that species becomes extinct.

fossil The shape or remains of a plant or animal that died long ago, hardened and preserved in rock

fossil fuel A fuel, such as coal, oil or gas, made from *fossil* remains of living things

geologists Scientists who study what the Earth is made of, how it formed and how it is changing

glacier A mass of ice that flows very slowly downhill

globe A spherical map

gravity The force of two objects pulling towards each other; the force that keeps Earth in *orbit* around the *Sun*

habitat The place where an animal or plant *species* lives

humidity The amount of water in the air

ice age A period when the Earth is much colder than average. There have been several major ice ages in Earth's history.

ice caps Large areas of ice, at the North and South *poles*

lava Hot, molten rock which bursts or flows out of *volcanoes*

magma Hot, molten rock inside Earth

magnet An object that has a magnetic force – an invisible force that attracts other objects

magnetic field The area around a *magnet*,

such as Planet Earth, in which objects are affected by that magnet's force

mantle The thick layer of rock under Earth's *crust*. Most of it is solid but some is *magma*.

marine Relating to the sea

meteorite A rock from space that has landed on the surface of a planet or moon

meteorologists Experts in the study and forecasting of the weather

microscopic Very small; visible only when viewed through a microscope

migration Movement from one place to another. Many animals migrate each season to find food.

mineral A substance found in rocks on Earth, such as salt, diamond or quartz

nutrients The parts of food and drink that a living thing absorbs to stay alive

oceanographers Scientists who study the oceans and the things that live in them

orbit To travel through space around another, larger object

ore Rocks from which *minerals*, especially metals, can be extracted

organism Any living thing

ozone A type of oxygen in which each molecule contains three oxygen atoms instead of two

ozone layer A layer of *ozone* in Earth's atmosphere, which protects living things from the *Sun*'s rays

Pangea A huge *continent* that existed on Earth 200-300 million years ago

permafrost A layer of the ground that is permanently frozen

petrified Turned to stone

photosynthesis The way in which plants and trees convert sunlight into energy

plateau An area of flat, high ground

poles The northern and southern extremes of Earth, which are farthest away from the *Equator*

pollution Harmful substances, such as waste, dirt and exhaust from cars, that are introduced into the *environment*

population The number of people, animals or plants living in a particular place

radiation Particles or rays of energy, including heat and light, given off by a substance or object

satellite An object, natural or built by humans, that *orbits* a planet

sedimentary rock Rock made up of particles of sand, mud and other debris that have settled on land or under water and been squashed down to form hard rock

solar system, the The group of planets, moons and *asteroids* that orbit the *Sun*

species A type of plant, animal or other living thing

star An enormous object in space that radiates powerful heat and light

Sun, the The *star* in the middle of our *solar system*

tectonic plates Large pieces of land that make up the Earth's *crust* and upper *mantle*

tide The daily rise and fall of the sea, caused by the Moon's *gravity*

time zone A region where the same standard time is used

tsunami A giant wave caused by an extreme movement on the seabed

universe, the Everything in time and space

volcano A cone-shaped landform created as *lava* and ash collect during an *eruption* around a hole in Earth's *crust*

Index

Making this book...
took a team of armchair explorers.

Research and writing:
Jerome Martin, Darran Stobbart, Alice James,
Tom Mumbray, Alex Frith and Rose Hall

Layout and design:
Jenny Offley, Lenka Hrehova, Tilly Kitching,
Helen Cooke and Jamie Ball

Illustration:
Federico Mariani,
Parko Polo and
Dale Edwin Murray

Series editor: Ruth Brocklehurst
Series designer: Stephen Moncrieff
Expert advisor: Dr. Roger Trend

This edition first published in 2021 by Usborne Publishing Limited, Usborne House, 83–85 Saffron Hill, London, EC1N 8RT, United Kingdom. usborne.com Copyright © 2021, 2019 Usborne Publishing Limited. The name Usborne and the Balloon logo are registered Trade Marks of Usborne Publishing Limited. All rights reserved. No part of this publication may be reproduced, stored in any retrieval system, or transmitted in any form or by any means without the prior permission of the publisher. UE. First published in America 2019. This edition published 2023.